"*Courageous Cultures* offers a compelling and actionable roadmap for business leaders to tap into the energy and wisdom lying just below the surface within their own organizations. With data-backed insights and a straightforward approach, *Courageous Cultures* will help leaders create a strong culture where the great ideas brewing in the minds of knowledgeable frontline workers are always welcomed and fully encouraged by every manager. In a business environment faced with continually shifting customer expectations and rapidly changing competitive forces, no leader should be without this valuable resource."

—RANDY OOSTRA, President and CEO
of ProMedica Health System

"In today's uncertain times, courage is indispensable to effective leadership. Without a culture of courage, leaders cannot lead organizations to seize opportunities for growth that change brings. This book offers simple steps on how leaders can nurture a bold organizational culture that encourages people to speak up, take smart risks, innovate, become problem solvers, and seize competitive advantage in a fast-transforming business environment."

—SUNIL PRASHARA, President and Chief Executive
Officer of Project Management Institute

"Don't we all want to promote a culture where our employees are able to speak up, speak truth, solve problems and hold each other accountable? In *Courageous Cultures*, Karin and David use storytelling and examples to share the formula organizations need to 'Own the UGLY' and create a culture where employees do not have a fear of speaking up and can take organizations to new heights."

—KYE MITCHELL, Chief Operations Officer of Kforce

"In a world of accelerating disruption, Karin and David provide powerful tools to tap into the innovative and problem-solving capacity of every employee. No grandiose, glamorous, otherworld theory here; *Courageous Cultures* is a compendium of straightforward, proven, practical ideas and solutions. Read the book, and up your game."

—WHITNEY JOHNSON, award-winning author of
Disrupt Yourself and *Build an A Team*

"Trust is the currency of business. In *Courageous Cultures*, Karin and David give you invaluable tools and the road map to leverage trust and transform your results to build a twenty-first century organization."

—DAVID HORSAGER, CEO of Trust Edge Leadership
Institute and bestselling author

"Karin Hurt and David Dye masterfully unearth an invaluable competitive advantage for any company—a culture that promotes employee voice, honesty, and transparency. This book goes beyond theory to provide actionable advice that delivers results."

—ERIC GEORGE, MD, Founder and CEO of ERG Enterprises
and author of *We: Ditch the Me Mindset and Change the World*

"Don't miss out on the opportunity to create an open and fearless culture. *Courageous Cultures* is a timely and practical approach for business leaders and managers to create a positive culture where innovation and commitment will soar! You will be amazed at the possibilities when your employees feel truly empowered to share their ideas and solve problems."

—JEANNE MARTEL, CEO and Cofounder of ClinicalMind

COURAGEOUS CULTURES

How to
Build Teams of
Microinnovators,
Problem Solvers,
and Customer
Advocates

KARIN HURT & DAVID DYE

HARPERCOLLINS
LEADERSHIP

AN IMPRINT OF HARPERCOLLINS

Published by HarperCollins Leadership, an imprint of HarperCollins Focus LLC.
Any internet addresses, phone numbers, or company or product information printed
in this book are offered as a resource and are not intended in any way to be or to
imply an endorsement by HarperCollins Leadership, nor does HarperCollins
Leadership vouch for the existence, content, or services of these sites,
phone numbers, companies, or products beyond the life of this book.

ISBN 978-1-4002-1954-4 (eBook)
ISBN 978-1-4002-1953-7 (HC)

Library of Congress Control Number: 2020930371

Printed in the United States of America
20 21 22 23   LSC   10 9 8 7 6 5 4 3 2 1

To our children, Averie, Ben, and Sebastian
for the courage to believe, work, and
create a better tomorrow.

Contents

Foreword

Why Voice Matters More Than Ever . . .
and How to Make It Real

AMY C. EDMONDSON
Novartis Professor of Leadership and Management
Harvard Business School

was honored to be asked to write a foreword for this timely and practical book. The book is *timely* given the recent headline-grabbing corporate failures that can be traced in part to employee silence when voice was surely possible. At the same time, the *#MeToo* movement brought home the reality of sustained harassment and abuse for an unimaginable number of women in the workplace. When speaking up is thwarted, problems fester and have the chance to turn into major failures. This book's focus on how to build a workplace culture where employees can speak up—despite the very human fear of doing so—has thus never been more important than it is today. The book is *practical* because the authors equip readers with a series of simple exercises that they can use to build a culture in which people do speak up—and do so in ways that allow thoughtful listening and action on the part of leaders and coworkers.

We don't have to look far to find corporate failures to analyze. Notably, the fatal accidents of two 737 Max jets in October of 2018 and March of 2019 stand as stark reminders of the challenge of employee voice—even in high-risk industries. Understandably, these events led to intense scrutiny of Boeing production facilities, and in mid-2019 news began to emerge that workers in the Boeing 787 Dreamliner plant in South Carolina felt pushed to maintain an overly ambitious production schedule and were fearful of losing their jobs if they raised quality concerns. Although not the facility where the ill-fated 737s were produced, the South Carolina workers' experience presented a textbook case of a widespread belief among employees that speaking up will trigger retribution rather than appreciation. The accidents and the resulting media attention created a wake-up call for Boeing, culminating in the firing of its CEO in late December of 2019. What was required at the company was far more than technical fixes. Boeing, like so many organizations today, was in need of a massive culture change. Lacking what Karin Hurt and David Dye call a courageous culture, Boeing was at grave risk of missing errors and improvement opportunities alike.

WHY IS IT HARD TO SPEAK UP AT WORK?

To understand why a courageous culture is so necessary—and why it is such hard work to bring it about—we must first consider how worker silence can prevail even when a product is directly and obviously related to human safety. How is it that preventable mishaps can happen—as they did at Boeing—when so very much is at stake?

The answer lies in our shared psychology. We human beings are finely attuned to risk. Now, that ought to work in our favor, especially when it comes to things like engineering safety systems for airplanes or preventing wrong-site surgery in hospitals. The trouble is, we're attuned primarily to *interpersonal* risk rather than technical risk.

It's human nature. We don't want to ruffle feathers. We don't want to be the Cassandra bringing bad news—instinctively appreciating that messengers get shot, even when they're "just the messenger." We don't want to be thought of as stupid when we say: "I just don't see how this is going to work." We don't want a dressing-down when we point out a quality problem. Even in the absence of bullies—or of bosses sending a message loud and clear that dissenting views or pushback are unwelcome—people naturally assume that criticism is rude, half-baked ideas are unwelcome, and requests for help will trigger disdain.

Human beings spontaneously overvalue maintaining a sense of comfort, security, and belonging in the moment, and spontaneously undervalue the vague, probably-won't-happen-anyway, potential failures that might unfold in the future. Psychologists have a term for this bias—*discounting the future*—and it makes it easy for us to hold back on speaking up even when human safety is at risk.

On top of that, the incentives in most workplaces conspire against employees speaking up and against managers actually hearing them. As Bob Sutton at Stanford puts it, "bosses live in a fool's paradise," often of their own making.[1] The so called "mum effect" leads subordinates to soften bad news, or withhold it altogether, such that the higher you go up the corporate ranks, the rosier the picture can seem.[2]

COURAGE OR PSYCHOLOGICAL SAFETY?

Even before the welcome publication of this book, courage has been gaining attention in the management literature. We can safely say that courage at work has never been more desirable—or more challenging—and, as a growing number of people contemplate the challenge of speaking up at work, the related concept of psychological safety has received an explosion of interest in both the academic and practitioner management literatures. Mentions of "psychological safety" have grown exponentially;[3] my own recent book on the subject, *The Fearless Organization*, has been unexpectedly popular. This interest reflects, I believe, growing recognition that today's workplaces require people to collaborate, solve problems, and respond to unexpected challenges. Doing all of those activities well requires speaking up openly and without hesitation. Whether leading a team in the office or caring for patients in the hospital, psychological safety helps people communicate, experiment, and speak up.[4]

Within this active conversation about speaking up, we find understandable confusion about the relationship between psychological safety and courage. Does psychological safety take away the need for courage? Or does courage take away the need for psychological safety? The answer to both questions is a resounding "no." Psychological safety and courage are simply two sides of the same (immensely valuable) coin. Both are—and will continue to be—needed in a complex and uncertain world. Karin and David define a courageous culture in Chapter 1 of this book as a place where people speak up. I've defined a climate of psychological safety similarly—as an environment where people believe they can speak up.[5] In short, candor is as vital as it is challenging in the modern workplace. And fostering it will take a village-like multipronged effort.

Because of what we know about human psychology in hierarchies (and frankly, what social system isn't a hierarchy?), we cannot avoid the simple truth that speaking up is difficult. And so, facilitating voice requires working both sides of the equation. A climate of psychological safety is, for all practical purposes, one and the same as a courageous culture. Both terms describe workplaces where everyone understands that their voices are welcome. In these workplaces, speaking up is still not effortless (that could be asking too much!). But, in these workplaces, people nonetheless understand that voice is expected and valued, despite the pull toward silence.

The difference in emphasis between psychological safety and courageous cultures may be a meaningful one. When we emphasize psychological safety, we risk putting the burden squarely on the shoulders of leaders—whether of teams or organizations—to do what they can to create environments where others' voices can be heard. When we emphasize courage, in contrast, we put the spotlight on individuals—inviting them to step up and share what they see, wonder about, and worry about, despite the anxiety they may have about doing so, because of what's at stake. Here the risk could be seen as asking for heroics on the part of undervalued and at times under-rewarded employees everywhere.

It seems to me that any earnest effort to foster direct and timely voice at work will require emphasizing both sides of this precious coin at the same time. Leaders must do their part to encourage and invite voice. Everyone must do their part to speak up despite fear. Yet, it's undeniable that courage is more compelling. Who doesn't want to be seen as courageous?

For this reason alone, I'm excited about *Courageous Cultures*. Karin and David inject new energy—and new tools—into the Sisyphean quest to build organizations that can thrive in the 21st century by engaging the voices of all who work in them. The academic research is overwhelming: when people believe they can speak up at work, the learning, innovation, and performance of their organizations is greater. Teams and organizations in which people believe that their voices are welcome outperform their counterparts.[6]

MAKING IT REAL

Courageous Cultures offers a model for building energized teams of learners and problem solvers—a model that is desperately needed in today's workplace. At the very core of this model is a mindset that welcomes voice, whether it brings good news, bad news, or a puzzle. This mindset starts with curiosity and is fueled by passion about a compelling purpose. It naturally fosters the leadership behaviors that inspire and invite others' voices.

As you will read in the pages ahead, building a courageous culture starts with your own passionate commitment to doing so. You must start by sharing (and speaking often about) a clear, compelling mission. With that foundation, you can continue to nurture a courageous culture through issuing repeated and genuine invitations for voice—explicit requests in both formal team meetings and informal interactions. But without a commitment to responding in appreciative, productive, forward-looking ways, courage is quickly stifled. This book shows you how to do all three of these vital leadership activities, starting tomorrow. The framework offered by Karin and David mirrors the high-level advice you can find in prior writings on this topic[7] and, fortunately for readers, breaks this framework down into practical, sequential, actionable steps that can be taken in any workplace today.

Even if voice will always be challenging, leaders have access to a formula that works. *Courageous Cultures* offers such a formula, and leaders who adopt it with passionate intent will be poised to build the kinds of workplaces companies need and employees want.

CHAPTER 1

What Is a Courageous Culture?

"Why am I the only one who finds these issues? What's wrong with my managers? Why can't they see this stuff and fix it?"

"We've got so many ways for people to submit their ideas, why don't more people use them?"

"My direct reports are always out talking to employees, but why is it that all we get is a bunch of fluff?"

Have you ever found yourself asking these questions? You're walking around and discover a fantastic best practice—which everyone could benefit from—but no one knows about it, not even the folks five feet away from where you found it. Or you discover a glaring problem—which apparently has been going on for years—but no one bothered to tell you. Or you have a state-of-the-art suggestion system that's empty. We hear these challenges from leaders we work with all the time.

Do you know what's really interesting? When you talk to the frontline employees in these same organizations, you'll often hear statements like:

- "The only way to get the customer what they need is to use this workaround. I've been doing it for years, which is why my customers love me. It's not standard procedure, though, so I keep my head down and hope my boss doesn't notice."
- "They say they want our ideas, but nothing ever changes. I've stopped bothering."
- "Whenever a bigwig from HQ comes to do a focus group, my boss warns us to talk only about the good stuff so we don't look like we're complaining."

And we wonder, "Are you all working for the same company?" People have ideas. Leaders want to hear them. But somewhere it breaks down.

This disconnect stifles innovation, problem solving, and hampers delivering breakthrough results for your customers. Your success depends on quickly incorporating the best ideas from across your business, on understanding what's not working and how to make it better. But what if you never hear what's working well and what's broken?

For many companies, it's not senior leaders who fear making big go-no-go choices that stifle progress. Rather it's the exponential effect of thousands of small opportunities missed because people didn't speak up when they saw something stupid or didn't share their idea because it might not be well received. The best practices languish, unshared and unspoken. Why?

Because people are often discouraged for saying the wrong thing and not rewarded for saying the right thing—so they say nothing. The consequences can be dire: customers leave, problems multiply like the heads of the Hydra, and employees lose heart. The tragic truth is, most of the time, leaders think they're creating an open environment that encourages employees to speak up and are surprised when they learn that employees are holding back. Too often, both employees and leaders feel that no one cares about making things better.

WELCOME TO THE WORLD OF COURAGEOUS CULTURES

Instead of safe silence and frustrated leaders, what if you had a Courageous Culture? A culture where:

- Teams at every level of your business continually ask, "How can we make this better?"
- Leaders have the courage to ask what's not working and really listen.
- Everyone is confident to raise a hand on behalf of the customer and put purpose above politics.

What does it mean to have a Courageous Culture? Our favorite definition of culture comes from Seth Godin: "People like us do things like this."[1] It's that invisible force of mutual understanding and awareness that drives behavior. A Courageous Culture is a place where "people like us" speak up. We share ideas. We solve problems. The default is to contribute. It's a culture where silence isn't safe and effort is everything. Courageous Cultures go way beyond employee engagement. People are energized. They bring their whole selves to their work. Innovation isn't limited to the senior leadership team or R&D. Everyone innovates, every day.

This isn't a book about large-scale innovation, the groundbreaking shifts in direction to capture new markets, or building a game-changing product (though Courageous Cultures can do that too). It's about the daily innovation that improves your customers' experience today. The group that comes together and says "if we're serious about this, we've got to solve this problem" and then does. When you build a Courageous Culture, you'll see teams of Micro-innovators, Problem Solvers and Customer Advocates working together to make things better.

Throughout *Courageous Cultures*, we will introduce you to leaders, organizations, and teams that are committed to shifting their culture from safe silence to consistent contribution. Leaders like

Leon Haley Jr., MD, CEO of University Florida Health Jacksonville and dean of University of Florida COM-Jacksonville, who told us, "If we ignore our staff's ideas or disregard the potential of an idea they offer us, we're essentially inviting them to leave and take their idea to another hospital, clinic, or physician practice who will listen."

Cultures like that of Bridgewater Associates, one of the world's most successful hedge funds, with radical commitments to transparency, open-mindedness, and where speaking up with criticism isn't just allowed, it's expected.

Places like Trader Joe's, a grocer with the highest revenue per square foot and throngs of brand advocates, where continual improvement is fundamental and everyone does what it takes to serve the customer. Companies like Basecamp, whose founders, Jason Fried and David Hansson, are committed to a calm and productive workplace with courageous leaders who choose "calm over crazy."

Organizations like WellSpan Health, which is clear about its mission of health through exceptional care for all and which remains creatively curious about the best way to achieve it.

And businesses like Nestlé, which create a Courageous Culture through its commitment to diversity and inclusion.

You'll meet leaders who have built Courageous Cultures within their teams—even when their larger organization wasn't there yet. We'll share our own experiences building teams and cultures where people speak up, solve problems, and advocate for customers. And, perhaps most importantly, you'll meet many leaders[2] who are in the process of taking the next step to a Courageous Culture. We hope that these stories will inspire you with what's possible, give you practical examples to follow, and motivate you to build your own Courageous Culture.

Behind these stories, you will find the research. We set out to answer the questions we heard from those senior executives, to explore the gap between leaders' intentions and employees' experiences, and to find out, practically: How does courage show up at work and what makes it so challenging? How can leaders build teams of Microinnovators, Problem Solvers, and Customer Advocates? And finally, you're likely familiar with the concept of FOMO (Fear of Missing Out). Well, in our work with organizations around the world, we've encountered another "fear of"—Fear of Speaking Up, which we call FOSU. FOSU is the reluctance, hesitation, or outright fear that prevents people from sharing solutions, problems, and ideas. The final question we wanted to answer is what causes FOSU and how do leaders overcome it to build a Courageous Culture?

We worked with the University of Northern Colorado's Social Research Lab to answer these questions. We did quantitative and qualitative research studies and conducted interviews with leaders from around the world. We partnered with organizations in industries ranging from financial services to health care to defense industry engineers to dive deep and interview leaders at every level of the organization. We've asked participants at conferences where we speak and in the leadership workshops we conduct to talk with us about their experiences with courage at work.

What we learned was challenging, frustrating, and encouraging. We've written *Courageous Cultures* to distill this research and give you the road map to build a culture of microinnovation, problem solving, and customer advocacy. And while we're on that subject, let's take a moment to clarify what we mean when we talk about these innovative problem solvers.

TEAMS OF MICROINNOVATORS, PROBLEM SOLVERS, AND CUSTOMER ADVOCATES

A Microinnovator is the employee who consistently seeks out small but powerful ways to improve the business. She consistently wonders, "How can I make this easier, better, or faster?" Then she speaks up and shares what she's learned. He's the trainer who sees that new hires aren't retaining a key skill and, rather than rely on the curriculum he received, builds a new way to teach and evaluate it. She's the team member who sees a gap in the way data moves between two teams and builds a shared resource where both teams can quickly find what they need.

A Problem Solver is the employee who cares about what's not working and wants to make it better. He uncovers and speaks openly about what's not working and thinks critically about how to fix it. Problem Solvers care about the business, treat it as their own, and focus on solutions. She's the video producer at a rapidly growing marketing company who says, "We've got twenty-one different ways to manage projects and communicate with one another. We're wasting days and dollars duplicating effort or putting things in the wrong place. If we can narrow it down to three, we'll save money and be able to take on more clients." It's the team that can't get the information they need from their database, but they refuse to shrug and live with it. They roll up their sleeves and work together with IT and their manager until they find a solution.

A Customer Advocate is the employee who sees through your customers' eyes and speaks up on their behalf. Customers may include your clients, students, patients, citizens, or for internal corporate support roles, your colleagues. Customer Advocates actively look for ways to improve customers' experience and minimize customer frustrations. He's the nurse who observes that patients are more relaxed when they understand what is happening. He suggests that the clinic revise its procedures to begin every patient interaction with a statement of what's being done and why. She's the engineer who sees that by the time she receives the customer specs, the project is already behind the desired schedule. She recommends a new customer intake process that will help customers identify their needs much earlier in the process.

In our world of rapid change, a Courageous Culture is your competitive advantage. It ensures that your company is "sticky" for both customers and employees.

HOW TO USE THIS BOOK

We've written *Courageous Cultures* as an interactive team exercise. You can read the book straight through, but you'll get the most value when you and your team spend time with each chapter, complete the exercises together, discuss your opportunities, and implement the suggestions you'll find in the coming chapters.

The Road Ahead

In the next chapter, we discuss why a Courageous Culture is such a huge competitive advantage in an era of unprecedented change. In Chapter 3, we'll share the findings of our research into what keeps people from speaking up and then lay the foundations for what you can do to overcome that reluctance. In Chapters 4 and 5, the focus shifts to you and addressing the courage crushers you need to remove, followed by how you find the courage to credibly lead a Courageous Culture. In Chapter 6, you'll get a look at how Courageous Cultures work in practice and the elegant dance that makes them possible. Chapters 7–11 give you the tools to build a Courageous Culture. Chapters 12–14 answer questions about how to build systems and infrastructure that support Courageous Cultures, how to lead different types of challenging people, and how to help your managers lead a Courageous Culture.

As you read and discuss, you'll undoubtedly find ideas and techniques that you've already mastered and think, "Hah, they should have interviewed us for this chapter, we've got some great best practices!" Take time to celebrate those and find ways to reinforce that momentum. It will serve you well as you experiment with some of the new ideas that may be less familiar. We'd also love to hear about what you're doing. If you're up for sharing, please drop us a note to info@letsgrowleaders.com.

First Tracks

As you read *Courageous Cultures*, you will likely encounter ideas and techniques that feel like you're in uncharted territory. If you're a skier it might feel like you've ridden the first lift up the mountain after a great fresh night of snow and you get to make the first tracks in the deep powder. Or perhaps you had a similar feeling as a child jumping in the wet sand and making prints for your friends to follow. That's why we've designed this book with easy step-by-step First Tracks to get you started.

After we've laid the foundation in Chapters 1–5, Chapter 5 and the following chapters each include a First Tracks section at the end of the chapter to make it easy to get started on your Courageous Cultures journey. These are tools, best practices, and approaches you can use to build a Courageous Culture within your team. They are designed to build on one another, so we encourage you to do them sequentially. We're deliberate about inviting you to start small and build momentum as you go—picking a few areas to work on before thinking more broadly about your entire organization.

Your Free Strategy Guide

Finally, we want to invite you to download the free companion *Courageous Cultures Executive Strategy Guide*. You will find the First Tracks templates, additional discussion questions to engage your team, and more detail for the tools, best practices, and approaches you can use to build a Courageous Culture in your organization. You can download the *Executive Strategy Guide* at www.CourageousCulturesBook.com.

CHAPTER 2

The Power of Courageous Culture in a Gig Economy and AI Universe

The type of disruption most companies and government agencies are facing right now is a once-in-every-few-centuries-event. . . . More than just changes in technology, or channel, or competitors—it's all of them, all at once.

—STEVE BLANK, Professor of Entrepreneurship, Stanford[1]

I f your business includes work that is repetitive, routine, or structured in a predictable setting, you face competitive pressure to automate that work—if you haven't already. Technology is commoditizing many products and services, and the easy jobs are going away. According to a Pew research study,[2] experts predict robots and digital agents powered by artificial intelligence will significantly displace blue-collar and white-collar jobs by 2025.

More restaurants are moving toward tablet-based ordering; banks are closing branches as consumers prefer to do the easy transactions online; and even health care visits are being reduced by remote monitoring. In some circumstances, your customers may be delighted at the efficiency while you're also saving time and money. With so much being automated and quality service and products becoming the default price of admission, how do you differentiate your business from your competition?

The secret to surviving and thriving in the automation revolution is in what computers can't replace: human creativity, empathy, and critical thinking—especially in unpredictable environments. Leading in the automation revolution isn't about what you can control; it's about what you can create and contribute. How often are your employees speaking up with creativity, empathy, and problem solving? In too many businesses, the answer is "not nearly enough." If you want a competitive edge, you've got to tap into your team's human potential to do what humans do best—connect and create.

CONNECT

Computers may be able to "think," but we've never met one who can feel. Empathy can't be outsourced to computers. It's the humans who can pay close attention to the frustration points and figure out how to make it better. What ticks off your customers? What's annoying your team? Why are your peers so demoralized? And what really needs to be done to fix all that? The impact of AI isn't limited to employees. AI is changing how workers trust and engage with their managers—and connection is at the heart of these changes. Some workers prefer AI (think voice-assistant chatbots) to get information on topics like company policies, health insurance, and their remaining vacation days. These are areas where machines excel: providing accurate information quickly. But people still turn to human managers who can understand how they feel, coach them in their career, and build culture.[3] When connection matters, there's no substitute for a human being.

CREATE

Let's say your AI system tells you thirty-seven thousand of your customers used profanity to describe a recent transaction. Ouch. That's really important data, but what do you do next? It's the humans who can understand what's going on from a human perspective and work to solve the problem. Do your teams have the skills they need to contribute at that level?

When the easy work is automated, will your managers know how to draw out the best solutions from their teams? Do your front-line employees feel encouraged to speak up and share solutions? Do employees at all levels have the critical thinking skills to get to the root cause? If you're not sure, you're not alone. According to a recent PricewaterhouseCoopers CEO survey, 77 percent of CEOs[4] say they struggle to find the creativity and innovation they need. When you build a dynamic culture that leverages humanity to solve problems, respond to customers, and adapt to change, you build a strong foundation to survive—and thrive—in the automation revolution.

COMPETING FOR THE BEST TALENT

The humans on your team have more choices than ever, and the war for talent now includes the gig economy. From 25 to 30 percent of employees get income from short-term contracts or freelance work each month and the number is growing.[5] The gig economy shows every sign of expanding as employees value the flexibility and employers use gig workers to lower costs. And when it comes to future talent, Generation Z is now becoming known as the entrepreneurial generation. A Gallup study of fifth through twelfth graders reported that 77 percent want to be their own boss, 41 percent plan to become entrepreneurs, and almost half plan to invent something that changes the world.[6]

According to research done by Millennial Branding, 43 percent of college students would rather be an entrepreneur than have a job when they graduate. Why? Many young millennials and members of Gen Z watched their parents struggle through layoffs and frustration during the economic downturn, and they're a bit more cynical about working for an employer. Plus, they've got role models that prove you can be a great entrepreneur at a young age, and as "digital natives" they don't think twice about collaborating with people all over the globe to help them scale.

Today, insight into your company's culture and leadership is freely available online. The next job is just a click away, remote work lowers the barriers to changing jobs, and the ever-present lure of becoming your own boss whispers in the ear of your best talent. Your most courageous and creative prospective employees have no desire to sit in a cube and be told what to do. They want to connect, collaborate, and work on bigger problems. They want a voice. They want to think like an entrepreneur and learn skills that prepare them to compete in that world. The gig economy is your competition for talent.

In a gig economy and an AI universe with pervasive automation and technology, Courageous Cultures that feature social intelligence, creativity, and capable response to unpredictable environments are more valuable than ever—to differentiate your products or services and to attract and retain top talent.

COURAGEOUS CULTURES WHEN THERE'S NO ROOM FOR FAILURE

You might be wondering how Courageous Cultures work when people need to follow consistent processes. We hear this frequently: "I get that people don't want to sit in a cube and be told what to do—but that's why they call it work. And we work in a high-risk business. There's no margin for failure. If we screw up, people die." You can still find many examples of hierarchical, top-down, do-what-your-told management. You can also find hotels that haven't updated their furnishings in twenty years, but that doesn't mean you'd want to stay there. To be fair, though, there are many industries where consistent procedures save lives.

You don't want your air traffic controller experimenting with a new way to communicate with your pilot. You want your surgical team to follow their checklist: to make sure they're operating on the correct part of your body, that you've got the right anesthesia, and they've done everything to prevent infection. As one engineering executive in an industry where failure rates cannot exceed 0.0005 percent told us, "Risk is for weekends."

But consistently following procedures and minimizing risk doesn't mean blindly following orders. Quite the opposite. In these high-stakes, low-margin-for-error scenarios, Courageous Cultures are essential. As the stakes increase, the courage to raise issues before they become critical, to identify and solve defects, and to improve processes become even more important.

RIGHT FOR YOU?

If you're not in an industry directly affected by AI or the gig economy, you might wonder if a Courageous Culture makes sense for you. During the Great Recession, David was an executive with a charitable human service organization—about as far from AI as you can get—that served vulnerable populations of young people. They sustained their work with thousands of clients through generous financial contributions. Like most charitable organizations in 2008 and 2009, revenue contracted as the economy went into a tailspin.

At the same time, in response to a few cases of high-profile nonprofit organizations being exposed for poor financial management and fraud, granting agencies and donors demanded increased accountability, efficiency, and demonstrable results. While these trends ultimately improved many charitable organizations, they also put a heavy burden on cash-strapped organizations.

Faced with contracting revenue and the pressure to deliver more results, David's team found a way to nearly double the number of clients they served and improve their long-term results. But it wasn't because of David's idea. Two years earlier, an area director named Manuel had brought up an idea he and his team had been kicking around. David gave Manuel and his team the space and funds they needed to test out the idea. (We'll talk more about what to do with ideas that just might work in Chapter 10.) Within three years, Manuel's idea had scaled across the organization. Two years later it was adopted nationally—strengthening both the number of clients and the benefits they received.

Courageous Cultures work, but they also require work. As you read these early chapters and decide whether a Courageous Culture is right for you, we encourage you to answer the questions in the sidebar to help you consider the implications of changing technology, the changing workforce, and the kind of talent you need to attract, retain, and energize. In the next chapter, we'll dive more deeply into our Courageous Cultures research findings and set the foundation for the work ahead.

YOUR COMPANY IN AN AI UNIVERSE AND GIG ECONOMY

- How has technology impacted your customer experience (consider both external and internal customers)? What's better now; what's more challenging? How do you know?
- How will technology change your industry in the next three to five years? Five to ten years?
- How do the humans in your organization provide you with a distinct competitive advantage?
- How often are your employees speaking up with creativity, empathy, and problem solving?
- In the competition for talent, why would a prospective employee want to be a part of your culture?

CHAPTER 3

How Courage Works—
According to Research

Do I dare
Disturb the universe?
—T. S. ELIOT[1]

How does courage show up at work and what makes it so challenging? How can leaders build teams of Microinnovators, Problems Solvers, and Customer Advocates? It's one thing to have an opinion, but let's look at the data.

THE RESEARCH

Any discussion about courage at work quickly leads to Amy Edmondson. Edmondson is the Novartis Professor of Leadership and Management at the Harvard Business School and author of *The Fearless Organization: Creating Psychological Safety in the Workplace for Learning, Innovation, and Growth*. She describes how courage at work shows up when someone speaks up, challenges an idea, shares a different perspective, or reveals a mistake. Every one of these behaviors takes courage because, as Edmondson says, people default to "avoiding failure"—the loss of status, being labeled, or being viewed with disfavor that can result from speaking up.[2] Until you build a Courageous Culture, "people at work are vulnerable to a kind of implicit logic in which safe is simply better than sorry."[3]

But why is safe silence the default over consistent contribution? There are several reasons based in human psychology. One reason is that people tend to underestimate the future benefits of speaking up and overestimate the current risk, a concept psychologists call discounting the future.[4] It's easy for people to talk themselves out of speaking up or taking a risk for fear of looking stupid, making a wrong decision, or damaging their reputation. In a conversation with Jason Fried, cofounder of Basecamp and coauthor of *It Doesn't Have to Be Crazy at Work*, he explained that leaders who want people to contribute more ideas and creative problem solving need to understand that "it's hard for people to speak up—it's risky and there aren't a lot of incentives. You're putting yourself out there."

A second reason for safe silence and why it's often easier for people to talk themselves out of speaking up is a phenomenon psychologists call "diffusion of responsibility." This is when we see something but know other people see it too, so everyone assumes one of the other people will say something—and no one says anything.[5]

The third reason contributing to safe silence is that people tend to remember a very bad emotional experience more than a good one.[6] From a survival standpoint, this makes sense—focused attention on threats would help us avoid them in the future. As with other parts of our fight-or-flight responses, however, this tendency to remember the negative can prevent your team members from making positive contributions. They may have spoken up ten times in their career with positive results, but what they're most likely to remember is the one time they ran into an insecure manager who threatened their job for making him look bad.

These barriers to a Courageous Culture are natural tendencies, but they aren't set in stone. It's possible to change the culture and make the shift from safe silence to consistent contribution. We conducted our research to find out how these human tendencies show up and to find practical answers to help you build a Courageous Culture. We found five reasons that people don't speak up to contribute solutions, suggest microinnovations, or advocate for customers:

1. People don't think leadership wants their ideas.
2. No one asks.
3. They lack confidence to share.
4. They lack the skills to share effectively.
5. People don't think anything will happen, so they don't bother.

Let's look at each of these more closely.

1. People don't think leadership wants their ideas.

Executives, managers, and employees described what happened when they approached their boss with a great idea and an executable plan to improve the business. In many cases, their boss agreed their concept would work and was doable, but then they were told to go back and do things "the old way."

Forty-one percent of survey respondents said leadership doesn't value innovation, and 67 percent said leadership operates on the notion that "this is how we've always done it."

Why this matters: If employees don't think you really want their ideas, they won't bother to offer them. Your best thinkers are still thinking, but not about your business. They're starting a side gig, getting proficient at their hobby, or figuring out their next move.

2. No one asks.

One significant reason employees say they don't share what they think is that "no one asked." An astonishing 49 percent of employees surveyed said that they are not regularly asked for their ideas. And 35 percent said they were never asked for their ideas when initially trained for their role.

We heard from many managers who acknowledged that frontline employee microinnovations and customer service enhancements are vital for success, but they lack any regular way to ask for ideas.

Why this matters: You might think you're asking for ideas because you have an open-door policy or your company has a sophisticated suggestion system. But that's not enough for most employees to feel that they've been genuinely invited to contribute. Asking well requires a cadence of regularly asking for specific insights and ideas.

3. They lack confidence to share.

Forty percent of respondents said they don't feel confident sharing their ideas. That's not surprising considering how often managers (not just frontline employees) said they were told to keep their heads down and just do their work:

- "I didn't hire you to fix our company."
- "It's not your job to think about that."
- "I didn't ask you for your ideas."
- "The problem is that we have too many ideas. I don't want any more."

Why this matters: It's far easier to default to safe silence, and people remember the stressful times more than the time they spoke up and their idea was heard. There are a wide range of reasons why employees lose confidence, from toxic management behaviors to insecurities they're bringing with them from home. You need to be deliberate in understanding what's crushing people's courage and work to eliminate the real and imagined barriers preventing the humans on your team from contributing their best thinking.

4. They lack the skills to share effectively.

In many cases, employees simply don't know how to speak up in a way that can be heard. "In hindsight, I really hadn't done all the research." "I think I came into my new role a bit too gung ho. I had so many ideas—I think they thought I was cocky and critical."

Interestingly, 45 percent said there's currently no training available at their organization for problem solving and critical thinking.

Why this matters: Even if you're hiring experienced managers, chances are they haven't been trained to think critically, solve complex problems, or to encourage microinnovation and problem solving on their teams. And these skills are not intuitive for most people. If you want people to proactively identify and solve problems or find more innovative solutions, you've got to train them. If you want people to advocate for the customer, you need to give them the skills to know how to do that well from a balanced business perspective and give them parameters to help guide their decision-making.

5. People don't think anything will happen, so they don't bother.

One of the most significant issues, even in some of the highest performing organizations, is that people are convinced their ideas will be ignored. We heard from many managers who echoed this financial services executive:

> People bring up something once or twice. If it isn't acknowledged then we'll invariably come across an issue that's been out there for a while. We'll say, "Oh my gosh, why didn't we see this?" And we'll hear back, "Oh, we did see it, but we told so-and-so and he didn't do anything with it."

Fifty percent of the employees we surveyed said they believe that if they share an idea, it won't be taken seriously. And the number one reason people said they would keep a microinnovation to themselves (56 percent) is concern that they would not get credit for their idea.

Why this matters: You may be asking for ideas and even doing something with them, but if there's no feedback loop, employees will assume nothing is happening. And no one wants to make contributions that aren't recognized or valued. It's human nature to stop trying and redirect energy where you believe it will do some good. Our research is filled with examples of smart, creative people, even at the executive level, who made deliberate decisions to stop bringing new ideas because they felt it was a waste of time.

WHAT COUNTS AS COURAGE?

In addition to our quantitative research, we've consistently asked executives, managers, and frontline employees in every Courageous Cultures program we deliver: What's the most courageous act you ever did at work? We have asked this question of participants from Africa, Europe, the Middle East, Asia, and the United States. The answers are remarkably consistent:

- "I stood up to my boss."
- "I managed out a poor performer."
- "I shared truthful information no one wanted to hear."
- "I defended a coworker against a bully."
- "I argued an unpopular point of view."
- "I walked away from a bad situation."
- "I advocated for my career."
- "I fired a customer."
- "I went back to school."
- "I took a new position."

Most of these stories are not Courage with a capital *C*—the front-page news stories of whistle-blowing and confronting massive ethical breeches with career-threatening consequences. They are stories of courage with a lowercase *c*—choices to take a small, uncomfortable risk for the good of the business, team, or customer.

When we ask, "How did this courageous act make you feel?" the answers are also consistent:

- "Fantastic."
- "Relieved."
- "Strong."
- "Proud."
- "Stupid that I waited so long."

Small acts of courage compound to build innovation, problem solving, and superior customer experience at a massive level. That's the power of a Courageous Culture.

SMALL ACTS OF COURAGE SET THE FOUNDATION FOR COURAGEOUS CULTURES

So where do you start? What are the small-*c* courageous acts that lay the foundation?

Show a Bit of Vulnerability

Vulnerability builds trust. Your employees want to know they're working for a human being. Have the courage to let people see a bit more of who you really are and to admit when you're wrong or don't have all the answers. Healthy vulnerability builds trust and connection.

Manage Performance

Nothing drives high performers crazier than a boss who looks the other way and lets slackers slide. Have the courage to provide consistent performance feedback and address performance issues directly. When you do this early and often, the chances of you having to do the really tough stuff—like fire the guy—reduce significantly.

Advocate for Your Team

When employees complain that "my boss is a wuss," it's often because their boss won't advocate for the team's ideas or needs—even when they claim to agree. The minute their boss or a peer asks for more clarification or challenges an idea, they back down. If you can't influence others, your team will wonder why they need you.

Experiment

Another huge reason employees tell us their boss lacks courage is their boss's unwillingness to experiment with new ideas or approaches. If "It ain't broke, don't fix it" is your favorite mantra, learning the art of a well-run pilot program can go a long way in increasing your courage while reducing your stress.

Make Timely Decisions

No one wants to work for a waffler. Have the courage to make decisions and stick to them. If you struggle with this, get your team to help you.

Share Credit

One of the most surprising findings in our research was that a primary reason people are reluctant to share ideas is because they won't get the credit. A surefire way to stunt the growth of a creative culture is to steal the credit. When in doubt, credit the team.

SILENCE AFFECTS YOUR BOTTOM LINE

As long as employees remain silent, companies will lose money on flawed projects, innovations that never happen, and subpar customer service. These companies are also likely to see lower morale and higher turnover rates because teams feel discouraged about expressing opinions. The same dynamic applies in nonprofit businesses where efficiencies that serve clients and save money are vital for survival.

Gallup's data reveals that a mere three out of ten US workers strongly agree that their opinions seem to count at work. But by moving that ratio to six in ten employees, organizations "could realize a 27% reduction in turnover, a 40% reduction in safety incidents, and a 12% increase in productivity."[7] Simply put: the ideas people hold back are not trivial. And the majority of these ideas are not self-serving (kombucha on tap or foosball tables in the break room). In fact, when we asked about the suggestions they would share, respondents' most common responses would improve their company's:

- Efficiency in a process.
- Employee performance.
- Customer service.

And in tight labor economies, don't ignore the impact on retention. Fifty-five percent of our respondents said they would search for a new job if their voice wasn't heard. And 67 percent said that their leadership's response to idea sharing definitely impacts their desire to stay in their job. A significant body of research finds that when people feel they can speak up, contribute, and share problems, they're more satisfied, less likely to quit, and their performance improves.[8]

HOW TO MAKE COURAGE WORK

According to Edmondson, "Psychological safety is present when colleagues trust and respect each other and feel able—even obligated—to be candid."[9] That's the shift: not just "able" to tell their truth or contribute an idea, but "obligated." Cultural courage makes sharing and speaking up the norm, not just a behavior to be tolerated. The paradox of truly Courageous Cultures is that they require less daily courage for routine conversations.

Where does that trust start?

It starts with you. It takes courage to change a culture. This is the real work of leadership: the courage to change, to confront, to be vulnerable. Your courage activates the transformation to a Courageous Culture in which everyone knows their ideas are needed, valued, and implemented because leaders at every level regularly ask, respond, and equip employees to innovate, exchange best practices, and speak up on behalf of their customers.

In the next chapter, you'll decide whether a Courageous Culture is right for you and explore some of the toxic courage crushers you must eliminate before attempting to tap into people's most innovative thinking. In Chapter 5, you'll begin to create your own narrative around courage and fear, and then learn how to leverage your stories to inspire and build more courageous teams.

CHAPTER 4

Overcoming Courage Crushers, Common Mistakes, and Other Barriers to Courageous Culture

A doctor was trying to do an experimental procedure I knew could hurt a child (and was also against the parent's consent), so I blocked the door.

—PEDIATRIC NURSE

Jane, a committed nurse in one of our high-potential programs, shared the exhausting list of daily stupidity she faced from a bullying, narcissistic doctor—just to get her job done. She felt like every day was a courageous battle to advocate for her patients' needs. Her requests were met with sarcasm and microretaliation. She said that the administration knew of his antics but looked the other way because he was renowned in his field. The other participants in the session corroborated her story with frustrated nods. "That's why we have Fear of Speaking Up—you can't change a guy like him. And he's just one of many."

"Why do you stay?" Karin asked.

Jane's eyes welled up (as did Karin's and pretty much everyone else's in the room). "I just care so deeply about the patients. They're just very sick kids who need someone paying attention who cares."

Jane eventually left for another role where her passion and commitment were appreciated. That department lost a remarkable nurse. You can't possibly build a Courageous Culture if you tolerate even one guy like that—word spreads fast. Your Janes will go elsewhere.

And Jane's not alone. When people hear of our research, many share their stories of difficult situations where they had to overcome a toxic situation.

- "My boss was exaggerating the numbers to our leadership team. I held fast to the truth."
- "I stood up to a boss who was trying to bully me."
- "I called ethics because I was tired of all the screaming. And then I got retaliated against for calling ethics."
- "They asked me to tell the truth about the CEO's behavior. I did and he was fired."
- "My integrity clashed with the executive team's direction, so I quit."

Sobering answers, aren't they? When people spend their courage reserves just getting past the bad stuff, there's no energy left for the courage your business needs most—creative problem solving and microinnovation.

For most people, innovation takes energy and courage—the courage to be vulnerable, to risk rejection from their peers, or to invite uncertainty. Your people can make that effort only a limited number of times before they're done. The more courage they use to address injustice, toxic leadership, needless politics, or poor decision-making, the less energy they'll have to spend on what really matters. You won't get any of the courage you need to serve your customers or build your business if it takes a heroic effort just to fight against an existing caustic culture. To build a culture that leverages and amplifies every act of courage from every team member, start with a foundation of safety and clarity.

If you're serious about building a Courageous Culture, you can't tolerate even an ounce of harassment or bullying—from anyone, but especially from anyone in a management or leadership role (even if they're otherwise rock star performers). If it takes a week's supply of courage for an employee just to show up for another day, you're wasting money and talent.

BEYOND "ME TOO" AND OTHER INJUSTICE

It's interesting: when we are interviewed about our Courageous Cultures research, one of the first topics reporters ask about is sexual harassment and bullying. "Oh, FOSU, you mean like in the 'me too' movement? Yeah, let's talk about that!"

Actually, no. If you've got a culture rampant with sexual harassment and bullying, you're not ready for any of the techniques in this book. You can't possibly encourage innovation and problem solving when you haven't solved the most fundamental problems: when people don't feel safe and don't know unequivocally that you value them at the most basic human level.

Before you start any of this, carefully examine your systems and infrastructure for injustice or unintended consequences that prevent people from focusing on the work that matters most. Spend time with your frontline employees and really listen to what they experience every day. Ask courageous questions (see Chapter 8) that give them an opportunity to tell you what really happens. Take the comments in your employee surveys seriously. For every employee that spoke up, there's likely another who blew it off or stayed silent.

SHAMING, BLAMING, AND INTIMIDATION

When you're looking to build a Courageous Culture, the behavior of *every* leader matters. We talk to so many senior leaders who convince themselves that they must tolerate the bullying or demeaning and intimidating behavior of an executive or middle manager because of "all the other things they bring to the table" (such as innovation, deep customer relationships, the biggest sales funnel). And then they tell us "they're too valuable to fire."

If this sounds familiar, think about the messages leaving a toxic leader in place is sending to your team. First, you've told your team that you lack courage. You're not a strong enough leader to create a Courageous Culture. Next, you've told your team members that you don't value them. If you did value them, you would ensure they were treated humanely. Finally, you've told everyone that this kind of abuse, harassment, and bullying is okay.

You've planted seeds for even more chaos and disruption. We've had countless managers raise their hands in our training sessions and say, "Well, this all sounds great, but they're not serious about that here. Otherwise, [insert toxic leader's name here] would not be so successful. It's sad but that's what it takes to get ahead around here."

Remember how negative memories linger longer then the positive ones? Even one bad actor will be enough for many employees to see that this is the way "people like us"—or the people we aspire to be like—are encouraged to act. And they will see this even if they're surrounded by a dozen other leaders proactively working to build the culture they want.

The three most toxic behaviors we hear being tolerated (and even rewarded) are shaming, blaming, and intimidation. It's the chief operating officer who projects a list of all her senior leaders in stack-ranked order on the screen at the company off-site gathering and then works her way through the list from the bottom up, sarcastically criticizing them in front of their peers and handing them a microphone to respond, as all their peers laugh nervously while silently praying they'll be spared next time.

Or the vice president who berates his direct reports for a strategic choice "they made" that didn't pan out, even though the VP was the one who made the final call despite the team's concerns and objections. Or the executive who flies around on the corporate jet and delivers fix-it-or-else ultimatums, overlooks all the great results, and leaves a wake of intimidation-induced frenzy—all to show how serious she is to make things better.

Shame, blame, and intimidation have no place in a Courageous Culture—and yet you might be surprised how frequently we encounter these counterproductive activities, even in organizations who invest in resources and systems to foster courage and innovation. Don't let one or two bullies undermine your Courageous Culture strategy.

OTHER MISTAKES

Toxic leadership behaviors are certainly the biggest courage crushers that sabotage a Courageous Culture, but there are also some other mistakes that get in the way.

Chronic Restructuring

"We've had another restructuring and now everything is in turmoil" is the most frequent frantic call we get from executives. Restructuring is often necessary and has many benefits if done at the right time for the right reasons, but don't underestimate the toll that it takes on clarity, curiosity, and courage. A new boss with new goals and new rules slows people down—and restructuring has a multiplier effect with many people in new roles with new teams and new managers. Everyone is on a deep search for clarity and FOSU feels like the safest bet until the dust settles. When the dust never settles, it's even easier to take a wait-and-see approach. Sometimes people are still waiting to see when the next restructure hits. So they wait some more. As a software development manager told us, "We've had two restructures in the past three years and are back where we started. It's created massive uncertainty—people wonder, 'If they couldn't get this right, what else isn't right?'"

Leadership Indecision

We frequently encounter managers who've made a career of executing well in a culture with well-defined processes but who don't know what to do with the "idea people" on their teams—so they shut them down. After all, innovation can be a distraction. And they may be proud of their no-failure track record—why take a risk now?

If you have a cadre of well-meaning managers who are scared to pull the trigger on a new idea, you'll need to help them work through their fear and teach them how to manage calculated risk taking. Do this before you work on the innovation and problem solving on the level below or you'll frustrate your teams as their microinnovations meet play-it-safe-managers. We'll give you more tools to help your managers lead Courageous Cultures in Chapter 13.

False Competition

It isn't the guy in the office next door who's your competition; it's mediocrity. And yet with stack ranks and performance potential grids it's easy to forget that. Recall that one of the biggest reasons people don't share ideas is that they worry they won't get the credit. In an environment with high internal competition, people are much more likely to keep best practices to themselves.

Poor Communication Infrastructure

One of the first observations we make in companies struggling to build an infrastructure of courage is poor communication. Meetings that should have been an email waste everyone's time; emails that should have been a conversation get lost in translation; or no one's talking about what really matters. There's lots of conversation with no action, and people move so fast they don't listen to one another.

IS A COURAGEOUS CULTURE RIGHT FOR YOU?

If you've gotten this far and are thinking, "I'm not sure a Courageous Culture is for us," you might be right. The techniques we suggest here require a foundation of trust. You or your team might not be ready. If your managers haven't mastered the fundamentals of managing high-performance teams, we'd encourage you to start with our first book, *Winning Well: A Manager's Guide to Getting Results—Without Losing Your Soul*,[1] before taking on these advanced culture-building techniques.

Or if you're an unapologetic micromanager, you'll likely frustrate your team if you head down this path only to pull back the reins. Better not to start. This book is for leaders who know the benefits of teams of Microinnovators, Problem Solvers, and Customer Advocates and who want a road map to make it happen.

CULTURAL OASIS

When we're talking about Courageous Cultures, people often ask us, "If my company isn't there yet, is it still possible to build a Courageous Culture on my team?"

It will be harder, but it is possible to create what we call a courageous cultural oasis, even within an old-school culture. It will require an extra dose of clarity on how what you do fits within the bigger picture. And you'll need to manage boundaries and support your team in knowing when to stand out and when to fit in.

One of our favorite examples of a leader who built a cultural oasis is a senior manager named Jamie Marsden. When you meet Jamie for the first time, you're struck by his warmth, the constant smile he has for the people around him, and how your ideas are met with an ebullient, "Brilliant!" spoken with a touch of his Scottish accent. He works in a very technical, high-pressure, fast-paced international industry that isn't known for its people-centered leadership.

In a conversation with Jamie, he described how he was invited to a discussion with senior leaders regarding the organization's employee retention challenges. Jamie told us:

> I raised the absolute critical importance of the relationship between the manager and employee, and the employee's experience of work through either good or bad management. I told them that as I was moving up into more senior leadership roles, I was struggling within the company to find people that I could go to, other managers, other leaders that had tried some of the things I was thinking of trying, to really get my team engaged and motivated. I suggested in that meeting that we should maybe get the managers together who are really passionate about being managers, who really look after their people, and work on their development and growth and help them to succeed. It's not easy being a manager, so I thought we could just share ideas, share examples of what's worked, best practices, and just keep each other motivated.

To Jamie's surprise, the senior leaders sanctioned the idea and Jamie found himself with permission to start a group focused on human-centered leadership. The group started with a monthly meeting of forty handpicked managers who displayed a passion for leading their people. The community, a voluntary group within the larger company, has grown to include four hundred participants and continues to feature exchanges of best practices and mutual encouragement, and invites external speakers.

When we asked Jamie about what it took to turn his idea into reality, he admitted that it took a tremendous amount of work.

> I did a lot of it outside of my normal work, but I couldn't have done it alone. The first thing I did was talk with three other people who I knew were on the same wavelength. That's what I would tell anyone who has an idea and you're

not sure what to do next. Find the like-minded people and work together.

We've had the opportunity to speak and spend a day with members of the community Jamie and his colleagues started. It is a fantastic example of how you can build a cultural oasis—and how, over time, that oasis can transform the larger culture.

Sometimes you can build a cultural oasis within your team with a single act of shared courage. David was invited to meet with CultureX, a community of managers and individual contributors in Denver, Colorado, who were committed to building positive culture in their respective organizations. That night he met Ivan, a senior product manager who shared his experience creating a cultural oasis.

My team and I were under the gun to get a new product launched. Everyone was working long days and we were stressed. But I had this team member who was very smart. He was easily the most productive person on the team in terms of what he produced. But he was a total jerk. He bullied everyone to get his way. He cussed out anyone who asked him for anything. And when you asked him to do something he didn't want to do, he'd throw a tantrum. Sometimes he'd literally throw things—whatever was handy, a mug, potted plant, whatever. We'd tried to work with him, performance improvement plans and all that, but nothing changed.

I'd finally had enough, so I went to my director and told him that we had to get rid of this guy. My director understood—he'd had to deal with this guy more than once, but here's what he said. He told me, "Ivan, I get it. I'm not going to tell you not to fire him. It's your call. But I've also got to tell you that, no matter what, you've got to meet the deadline—and if you do let him go, you're not going to get anyone else before this has to be finished." So he basically just told me I was on my own. I swallowed hard and decided to fire the guy.

The next morning, I met with the team to tell them that the jerk was no longer working with us. Then I told them the situation: we wouldn't be getting any other help, he'd been our top producer—and we still had to meet the deadline.

When we talk about culture, I don't think I'll ever forget what happened next. The team pulled together. Everyone worked hard and supported each other, and without all that negativity on the team, we got way more done. We met the deadline easily—without him and without adding anyone else.

Whether your organization chooses to build a Courageous Culture, you have a choice about how you lead your team. We want to invite you—and Jamie and Ivan challenge you—to lead with courage.

COURAGEOUS CULTURE QUESTIONS TO CONSIDER

Before you read any further, we encourage you and your team to discuss these questions:

Why Build a Courageous Culture?

- Why do you want a Courageous Culture?
- What specific outcomes are you looking to achieve?
- How will you know you are successful?
- What scares you? Why?
- What hard choices must you be prepared to make?
- What support do you have? Who's with you? Who's not? Why?

Avoiding Courage Crushers

- What processes do you have in place to prevent (and make it easy to report) bullying and harassment?
- What do you do when a high performer regularly abuses or harasses other people?
- Which of these courage crushers is the biggest source of vulnerability for your organization?
- What behaviors will you have a zero tolerance for in your organization?
- Do your managers have the fundamental management and communication skills they need to implement a Courageous Culture?

CHAPTER 5

Navigate the Narrative

All courage is a threshold crossing. Often there is a choice: to enter the burning building or not, to speak the truth or not. . . . But there is another sort of courage we are talking about here—the kind when afterward, the courageous are puzzled to be singled out as brave. They often say, I had no choice.

—MARK NEPO, *The Book of Awakening*[1]

K arin was facilitating a leadership development program at a government agency with an interesting mix of scientists and administrators. About halfway through the program, one of the participants, Hope, expressed a concern: "I believe all these techniques will work for someone like Peter, but they would never work for me." Peter was a white male participant with impressive scientific credentials and a more powerful position in the organization. Hope believed Peter could speak up when she could not. She wasn't the only one who thought so. Many of the participants in the room had their own concerns about marginalized voices and the general silencing of dissent.

As discussion continued, numerous participants shared their experiences of being told to be quiet or spoke of the repercussions they felt when they brought up bad news. The stories were sad, compelling, and real. Every detail lingered in their memories as if the incidents had happened just yesterday. In reality, some of the stories were a decade old—and involved a peer or boss who was no longer around. Even so, the residual fear was palpable. There was a whole lot of FOSU in a culture that desperately needed the truth. There's no question that results suffered, projects took longer, and outcomes declined from the lack of speaking up.

Despite feeling like she didn't have a voice, Hope had spoken up—and she started a conversation. After listening to Hope and his other colleagues share their experiences of being silenced, Peter raised his hand.

I hear you. I do—I've also been told several times by my boss to keep quiet and not rock the boat. One time I saw several errors that I knew would delay the timeline of our project. I took them to my boss who told me under no circumstance was I to disclose the situation and make the team (or him) look bad. Several months later, the project was in trouble, and the department head, Joe, got involved. He asked why I hadn't said anything. I told him that I had but that it didn't go anywhere.

Joe coached me and said that in these situations it's important to put the project ahead of self-protection. He reminded me of what was at stake, the importance of our work, and that I can always come talk with him when I need to. I still respect the chain of command, but I do talk to Joe from time to time. My boss hates it when I go to Joe, but sometimes I have no choice except to do the right thing.

Soon after that, my boss, peers, and I were in a meeting with Joe. Joe told us how frustrated he was that people won't speak up. He looked at my boss and said, "Peter's the only one who does." Then he asked the rest of the team why they stayed silent when they knew there were issues, but everyone, including my boss, just stared at him blankly and didn't say a word.

After the meeting, my boss took me aside and said, "See, Joe wants you to stop speaking up! Now stop it."

I was like, "What? Were we just in the same meeting? That's not at all what he said." I insisted that my boss and I speak together with Joe to clarify what he wanted.

Joe was unequivocal: "I want Peter and everyone on this team to speak up. That's the only way we will know what's ever going on."

Peter slowly looked around the room at each of his colleagues and said, "It may not feel like it, but there are people who want to hear what you have to say." As Peter concluded this story, some of the participants looked thoughtful. Others nodded. But others looked dubious, because Hope was also right. It's easier for a guy like Peter to pull this off, and there's no guarantee that women, people of color, or employees with different credentials would have had the same experience as Peter. Then Peter began his second story.

About a year ago, one of our colleagues told me she thought I was a bully. I was shocked and hurt. I didn't see myself as a bully. I asked why she thought so. It came down to the fact that I was holding people accountable and that was uncomfortable.

Now, I have to hold people accountable to get the results we need. But I also knew that accountability is one thing but bullying is another. So I asked some of my other peers for their perspective.

Several of them said, "Oh yeah, sometimes you're a bully."

That's when I knew I needed to change. I dug deeper by asking more questions about how my behavior was being perceived and got some clues on how to change. I started listening more. I entered rooms more gently. I watched my tone and manner. No leadership work I've ever done has had a bigger effect on my influence. I'm still holding people accountable, but now I pay attention to my style. It's easier and better for all of us.

Peter paused and looked around the room.

Imagine if the woman who told me I was a bully had FOSU? If past experiences, like we've been talking about, had shut her down and she never told me I was coming across as a bully—would any of you have had the courage to call me out on my behavior?

He paused. No one answered.

She did all of us a favor by speaking up. *I'm a better leader because she had the courage to tell me what was happening.* I understand the culture we're in. There's some jerky behavior, but I've also got to say, we need people to speak up more often. Don't assume you won't be heard—some of the people you let get away with these behaviors may be as oblivious as I was. We have to talk about this stuff if we're serious about culture change. We're in this class because they want us to stand up as leaders.

It was a powerful moment.

Peter's vulnerability was transformative. Sharing his story—and the story of the woman who challenged him—created just enough safety for some of the participants to find the courage they needed to experiment with how they approached their work and their interaction with colleagues.

WHAT'S YOUR STORY?

The next step to create a Courageous Culture is to Navigate the Narrative. We all tell ourselves stories about what's happening, who we are, and what other people think about us. To Navigate the Narrative means that you pay attention to the stories you tell yourself, the stories your teams tell themselves, and consciously tap into the stories that reinforce your values, culture, and commitments. Courage starts with you—the courage to get real with yourself, acknowledge your internal stories, and ground yourself in the experiences that give you and your team confidence and courage. Then you'll be able to role model a Courageous Culture for everyone else.

Don't underestimate the role your personal courage plays in building a Courageous Culture for your team. Khalil Smith, head of the diversity and inclusion practice at the NeuroLeadership Institute, and his colleagues say it this way: "When voice becomes a priority for leaders, with the right habits and systems, it can become a non-heroic act for everyone to speak up, rippling out across all levels of the organization."[2] That "non-heroic act" translates to "culture"—people like us, doing things like this. Your leadership is the first step; you are the first person "doing things like this."

When it comes to summoning your own personal courage, it's helpful to get perspective on your experiences. Recall the brain's tendency to remember the details of a bad or traumatic experience more than a good one. You may have spoken up dozens of times, but it's the one time when your jerky boss embarrassed you in front of your peers that pops up as a warning siren reminding you that "it's safer to stay silent."

Each of the participants in that powerful conversation with Hope and Peter had stories from their experiences that influenced what they believed and how they acted on those beliefs. Hope told herself a story about speaking up. In her story, she believed her voice wouldn't change things (and that white men didn't have the same experiences). But then she did speak up, and now she has proof she can be heard. Navigating the Narrative means she would own that story and choose to live in it, remembering the power of her voice the next time it was needed.

Peter had his own stories (that his concerns merited discussion and that he was a decent, fair guy). Joe's support validated the first story despite his boss's opposition, but the second story didn't align with his behavior. Despite his intentions, his behaviors were sending a different message and he needed to change them if he wanted the story to be true. The courage to look unflinchingly at feedback that doesn't mesh with our view of ourselves is powerful. As Peter lived in that story, it brought him to a place where he could courageously invite his colleagues to join him in speaking up, even when it was difficult, and offer them hope that their words might be received.

Sadly, the opposite is far too common. One or two negative experiences with a bad manager, or bullying peer, will be enough "proof" for most people that speaking up isn't safe. People shut down and they stay "safe," which is further "proof" they made the right call. Of course, they will never know what would have happened if they made a different choice. So many of the scared managers we speak with are stuck in that cycle.

Peter described his courage as "having no choice" but to act on his values. Thankfully, his experience with Joe taught him that speaking up, though not easy, is safe enough. That positive experience bolstered his confidence not only to try again but to be more like Joe when receiving feedback that he'd rather not hear. Nothing builds confidence quicker than past success. Which stories do you tell yourself? What stories does your team live in?

NAVIGATE YOUR NARRATIVE

If nothing builds confidence faster than past success, how exactly do you Navigate the Narrative and ground yourself in the stories that will help you lead a Courageous Culture? Early in the conceptual stage of this book, we asked ourselves that same question. As we looked at how leaders and teams show up with courage in everyday situations, we went back to peers, direct reports, and bosses who at one time or another had remarked on our courage. Looking for hints to simplify courage and make it easier to teach, we asked them to recall the moments that made them think we were courageous. What we heard surprised us. We share a few of these stories here to demonstrate the power of reflecting on your own courageous stories and looking for the values that emerge. We will invite you to do the same in your initial First Tracks assignment at the end of this chapter.

One incident that several people mentioned to David when he asked about courageous moments involved poor behavior from someone with status and power. During his time as an executive leader at a national nonprofit, someone on David's board of directors, who was also one of the biggest funders, had a habit of treating staff disrespectfully. David and the board chair had both spoken with this donor about the behavior. They'd repeatedly asked him to respect the chain of communication and contact David or the board chair with any concerns or issues that he might have. (This is standard operating procedure for nonprofit organizations and associations.) They were diplomatic—funding is not easy to come by and the organization was growing, looking for every dollar they could find.

One day, David returned from a meeting, walked into the office, and found his executive assistant in tears. It turned out that the board member thought the executive assistant had made a mistake with marketing materials (she had not). He called her, yelling at her for the perceived mistake and belittling her competence. When David found out what had happened, he immediately wrote the board member, summarized the conversations they'd had previously, explained how his behavior was beneath his station, unprofessional, and destructive. David directed the staff not to accept any phone calls from this board member and told him that he was no longer welcome in the office without an appointment. David copied the board chair, apologized to his assistant for her experience, and went home.

As he drove home, David expected a phone call from his board. After all, he had just confronted their top financial supporter. Given the board member's personality and past behavior, it was likely that he would demand David's resignation or pull his funding. The financial fallout could be significant. Executives of any kind don't last long when funding declines. But the phone never rang. The next morning, the board member announced his resignation and reduced his contribution, but did not pull it entirely. The organization went on to successfully raise more funds and expand as it had hoped.

That is one example of the courageous moments our colleagues and mentors recalled. These courageous moments included advocating for employees, taking an unpopular stand, standing up to toxic people, or making a giant leap of faith. What surprised us about the times people remember us having courage is that these were not times we felt courageous. If you'd asked us how we felt in the moment, we might have said we were angry or concerned or even desperate. Talking about the incident we just described, David said, "I didn't feel brave—just angry." In our conversations with other leaders, a similar theme emerges. Courage doesn't always feel like courage. It often feels like something else.

Courage shows up in these moments where you choose to live according to your values. In Mark Nepo's quote that opens this chapter, he describes how people are often puzzled to be called courageous. If you've ever done something that others might not have done, but you did it feeling that "you had no choice," that's because you'd made the first choice much earlier in your life. At some point, you made a choice about what you value. About what's important and who you want to be. Every decision after that makes the next one easier. Until, at some point, it's not conscious courage; it's just you being you.

Of course, "just you being you" doesn't mean you can recklessly speak your truth. Karin's most regrettable moment in her career was when she lashed out in rage at a manager in another department who she felt was discriminating against one of her top performers because of race. She used words she regrets, at a decibel she regrets, at a place and time she regrets. She had the speaking-up part right, and her anger was justified. No regrets there. But how she spoke up and when she chose to do it completely derailed her ability to influence the situation and damaged her reputation. Karin learned so much from that regrettable moment. Courage also means that you know your triggers, you manage your emotions, and use them to take constructive action that creates real change.

To Navigate the Narrative means you identify the stories in which you are the best version of yourself or learned positive lessons, consciously choose to remember them, and use them to inform your choices today. It becomes easier to be that best version of yourself the next time. As you do, your commitment to your values grows stronger than your fear.

Not long after that outburst, Karin, her boss, and her boss's boss were flying around the country on a series of site visits to Karin's teams. During the visits, the most senior of the executives displayed what Karin considered to be toxic leadership that clashed with Karin's values, and she had a deep urge to provide feedback. The teams were doing some remarkable work, and she worried the executive's behavior would undo all the good progress. Her well-meaning boss cared deeply about Karin and her career. She saw the fury washing across Karin's face, took her aside, and said, "Karin, if you care about your career, you won't say a word."

Now, there's a difference between courage and stupidity, and tapping into the wisdom she'd gained from her earlier experience of reacting to perceived injustice without taking a moment to find the best approach, she heeded the advice and didn't say anything—at least in that moment. But on the flight home she took out her laptop and began writing down all of her leadership values. Then on the drive home, she called members of her own team to apologize for the executive's approach and reminded them that under no circumstances would she ever want to act like that and invited them to hold her accountable, if she did. She reminded them that she wouldn't tolerate behaviors like that from any member of her team either. She reinforced what "people like us" do on her team—even if others choose differently. And then, that Sunday morning, Karin started the *Let's Grow Leaders* blog, sharing everything she knew about how to get results and be a decent human being, with an occasional rant about toxic leaders.

Sometimes it's not a matter of if you should speak up, but how. That list of values she wrote on the plane, and the blog that followed, were the start of the platform that allows us to serve leaders around the world to help them get breakthrough results and stay connected to their values.

CONTINUING THE STORY

Once you've tapped into your courage and helped your team to recognize theirs, it's time to continue the story. How will you expand your courage and professional influence? One of the most effective ways to build and demonstrate courage is to intentionally stretch yourself. We heard a great version of this practice from Susie, a leader at a large consumer products company. The company developed a formal approach to help managers isolate and practice behaviors that would help them overcome their fears and improve their results.

They encouraged managers to pick one behavior. The chosen behavior had to meet three criteria:

1. It would help them improve their performance.
2. It had to be relatively simple to do.
3. It also needed to feel scary to the manager who chose it.

Once they'd chosen their behavior, they would practice it consistently every day for a limited time. For example, if a manager's fear of being underprepared led them to waste time overpreparing, they could take on the "one-hour prep time challenge," in which for two weeks, they would set a clock to limit themselves to one hour of preparation for meetings.

Or if a manager's fear of disappointing others led them to take on too many peripheral tasks, distracting them from their most important priorities, they could take on the "say it with your signature" challenge, spelling out their big three strategic priorities in their email signature, thus making it easier to open the discussion of why they sometimes had to say no.

These experiments are both easy and uncomfortable; that's their magic. They weren't long-term commitments, just focused efforts to try out a new behavior and observe the impact. When you and your managers take on miniexperiments like these, you continue the story you've chosen. Each subsequent act of courage comes more easily and you've modeled vulnerability and growth for your people. Remember, when your team can see your courage, it bolsters theirs.

FIRST TRACKS

Courage Map

We've come to your initial First Tracks assignment. You'll start your Courageous Culture journey by Navigating the Narrative with a Courage Map that helps you tap into your courage and give yourself the foundation you need to lead a cultural transformation.

OBJECTIVES:

- To reflect on your best experiences with courage to build confidence and lay the groundwork for your Courageous Culture strategy.
- To encourage conversation with your direct report team on what courage means and why it's important.
- To identify shared values and behaviors to ground your Courageous Cultures vision.

TIME REQUIRED:

About an hour depending on team size and length of conversation.

PROCESS:

1. To build your Courage Map, make a broad timeline of your career, thinking back to your early roles as well as more recent ones. Now think about the most courageous acts you did in these roles and lessons learned along the way. If you're like most of our clients, you'll recall some great ones that you haven't thought about in quite some time. If you're struggling to come up with at least three examples, do what we did: ask people who know you well to describe their memory of your most courageous act at work.

2. Once you've identified a minimum of three moments of courage, for each courageous act, ask yourself the following questions:

What motivated me to be courageous in this circumstance?
What did I expect to happen?
What actually happened as a result?
How do I feel about this incident?
What values did it reveal as important to me?
As a leader today, where would it be helpful to show up more like
this or with these values?

3. Look for the themes. What do you notice about yourself in these stories? What makes you proud? What is the essence of these stories that you hope to carry forward into your future stories? What lessons do you have to share with your team? How will you tell them?

4. Invite your direct report team to complete the exercise and schedule some time to discuss as a team. Have each person pick one story to share. What themes emerge? What do you notice about the underlying values of these choices? What are the key lessons from these stories you can leverage as you begin your work to build a more Courageous Culture?

CHAPTER 6

Courageous Culture in Action

Once the team understands that winning is equal parts belief
in the mission, developing strengths, and a relentless charge
towards the finish line success is inevitable.

—WAYNE SMITH, District Manager

As we reflected on our own experiences, did the research, studied best practices, and worked with clients who are building Courageous Cultures, we found a consistent pattern. Courageous Cultures require an elegant dance between two seemingly contradictory leadership characteristics: Clarity and Curiosity. To give you a sense of how Clarity and Curiosity interact in a Courageous Culture, we'll start with a case study from Karin and her sales team. After introducing the dilemma facing the team, you'll learn how Clarity and Curiosity work together, then dive more deeply into the specific tools and techniques they used to transform their results. In full transparency, we'd love to tell you that this turnaround resulted from a deliberate strategy—following the steps that we will introduce you to later. But the truth is, Karin and her team were learning as they went along.

Karin had just started a new role leading a retail sales team of twenty-two hundred people across three states. But her entire career up to that point had been in human resources, leadership development, training, and contact centers. The closest she'd come to sales was peddling Girl Scout cookies door to door as a child. Twelve of her fourteen district managers were men and all fourteen had extensive retail sales experience. Her predecessor was a well-loved and successful leader who had carefully groomed a replacement. Yes, the guy who didn't get the job was now her right-hand operations director.

One of the most vocal district managers didn't hold back his frustration and told her she was unqualified for the role—sharing that "this was clearly a diversity, succession-planning move." Naturally, she felt she had a lot to prove.

But that wasn't the most challenging part of the new sales role. Apple had recently entered into an exclusive arrangement to sell the iPhone with AT&T, Karin's team's biggest competitor. Customers were lining up at her stores to ask how soon they could leave for the competitor, and a new iPhone. Her sales team was demoralized. One team manager told her, "Lady, why don't you just go back to HR and convince them to lower our quotas. We've got nothing to sell."

What would you do? Your team doesn't trust you; they don't believe they can win; and they've got data that seem to prove it.

Fast-forward to when Karin was promoted out of that executive sales role. Her team led the nation in small- and medium-business sales, they'd won the company president's award for customer growth, and, perhaps most importantly, they'd reclaimed their mojo. They were selling again and they believed in themselves—all without selling the iPhone. How did they do it? In short, they built a Courageous Culture by mastering the Courageous Culture Cycle of Clarity and Curiosity.

THE COURAGEOUS CULTURE CYCLE

When we talk about Clarity and Curiosity, this isn't a simple "both/ and"—each of these elements takes center stage, never far apart, then gracefully yield to the other.

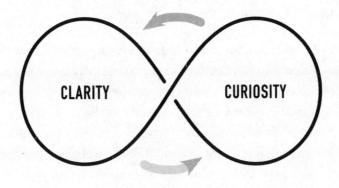

FIG. 6-1

Clarity

Clarity is focus, alignment, and doing what works. Clarity means that everyone in the organization has a shared understanding of what success looks like. Clarity ensures that your brand promise is kept in every interaction. People get where you are headed and why. Clarity contributes three critical elements to a Courageous Culture: safety, confidence, and direction. Clarity helps people speak up because they know what success looks like, what's required of them, and how they can contribute. Clarity produces confidence that you can take a good idea and make it happen. Finally, Clarity gives people a direction to focus their thinking, problem solving, and creativity.

In organizations with a strong commitment to Clarity:

- executives communicate a clear vision of the future and what success looks like;
- managers translate vision to behaviors and ensure all employees understand what they're doing, why they're doing it, and how their work fits in; and
- frontline employees know what to do and how to do it well.

Curiosity

Curiosity is questioning, exploring, and trying what's new. Curiosity means that everyone explores how to improve. People ask great questions and actively listen to one another. Curiosity ensures that your organization consistently becomes the best version of itself. Curiosity contributes to a Courageous Culture by shifting the culture from permission to intention. Solving problems and speaking up isn't just allowed—it's who you are and what you do.

In organizations with a strong commitment to Curiosity:

- executives look for suggestions, solicit ideas, and act on what they learn;
- managers are on the lookout for new ideas and best practices—when they see them, they share them; and
- frontline employees find and surface ways to improve the business and customer experience.

In many organizations, Clarity and Curiosity don't coexist. Leaders focus on one or the other and experience predictable challenges. When you embrace Clarity to the exclusion of Curiosity, you miss opportunities that are hiding in plain sight. Silos and internal competition creep in as forward motion grinds to a halt. FOSU becomes an epidemic as people become more reluctant to challenge the proven status quo. You often lose top talent who want to innovate and achieve breakthrough results. Ultimately, you have teams full of people who just want to be told what to do and aren't creating the future.

In contrast, when you embrace Curiosity to the exclusion of Clarity, you'll experience a different set of challenges. Your customers' experience of your brand fluctuates wildly. You can't scale and it can take forever to implement change or best practices. Once again, you lose top talent—this time because they get frustrated at your organization's inability to follow through and achieve results. You'll often see teams full of "lone rangers" who invent their own, often different, ways to do the work.

In contrast, when you build a Courageous Culture, you integrate Clarity and Curiosity. In the dance between the two, each characteristic takes the spotlight, but they're always holding hands. In the pages to come, we'll give you practical ways to balance the interplay between Clarity and Curiosity and share many real-world examples of businesses that balance these characteristics.

BEGIN WHERE YOU AREN'T

When you first encounter the Clarity-Curiosity dance, you may feel overwhelmed and wonder where to begin. In subsequent chapters we'll break down the behaviors and give you the tools you need to build your own teams of Microinnovators, Problem Solvers, and Customer Advocates. In the meantime, we invite you to begin where you aren't. If you do a reasonably good job getting everyone aligned around the same outcomes and everyone knows what success looks like, then focus on the Curiosity phase. If you've got a glorious mess of energized rock stars who all passionately do their own thing, simultaneously reinvent the wheel, and step on each other's toes, begin with Clarity. If you're unsure, focus first on what comes least naturally to your culture. Either way, you will be back to the other side of the dance before long.

THE DEMORALIZED SALES TEAM TURNAROUND

While you're thinking about where to begin, let's get back to Karin's sales team. How did they transform from a demoralized team that was bleeding customers to the competition into leading the nation in small- and medium-business sales and winning awards for customer growth?

Commit with Clarity

As she stepped into her new sales leadership role, Karin and her team were clear about two goals:

1. They had to make revenue and provide a best-in-class customer experience. They also had the benefit of clear corporate branding and operations.
2. They needed to inspire hope and possibility for their demoralized sales team.

Remember that when building a Courageous Culture, you want to "start where you aren't." The team had Clarity, so they moved to Curiosity.

Cultivate Curiosity

Karin looked at her sales team and said, "With twenty-two hundred people, someone must be selling something." She needed to figure out who and what they were doing to succeed. She asked for a list of the top twenty sales people and headed out on what you'll learn in Chapter 8 is a Curiosity Tour to look for best practices.

That's when she met Yomi. She watched Yomi interact with customers and noticed a consistent pattern: he asked every customer one question: "Where do you work?"

After watching him repeatedly ask this question, Karin talked with him. "Yomi, why do you do that? Is that just to build rapport?"

Oh, no, Karin. I ask where they work because I want to know if they own a small business. Those small business owners don't want an iPhone for their businesses—it's so new that businesspeople are worried about data security. They still

want the Blackberry or a push-to-talk-phone. When I find out
they own a business, I tell them all about our great new small-
business plans. I'm bringing over five, ten, and twenty lines at
a time. I'm making bank. My customers are thrilled and they
tell their friends to come see me.

Karin was excited and shared Yomi's best practice with a few of
her district managers, but most of them weren't as enthusiastic:
"Oh, Karin, Yomi is Yomi. He could sell ice to Eskimos. Business
customers don't want to come to a retail store to buy phones. We've
tried selling to small business before. It just doesn't work." Now, in
full disclosure, Karin had no idea if this was a good long-term strategy. But she knew this: if salespeople believe they can't sell, they
can't sell.

Respond with Regard

She also knew that the only way to create real change is one behavior at a time, so she did what you'll see in Chapter 9 is Respond with
Regard by testing the best practice. Karin got her team together for
a quick huddle: "I'm not saying that selling to small business will be
our new strategy. This might not work. But we've got to try. I'm
asking you to go all in to try Yomi's approach for one day."

When you're working with a discouraged team and you want to
increase requirements and accountability, it helps to also increase
the fun. That's what the district manager team did. The team agreed
to give it an enthusiastic full-court press the following Tuesday.
They would require every salesperson working that day to ask every
customer, "Where do you work?"

They made that Tuesday feel like a holiday, calling it "Small Business Madness Day." They mapped out a plan to ensure that between
Karin and her district manager team, all 110 stores would get a visit
during the twelve hours they were open that day. They brought Red
Bull and candy to build energy and excitement and personally mod-

eled the key behavior: ask every customer "where do you work?" They also asked the teams to decorate the stores with balloons, so the customers would sense something was different too. The whole day felt like a party.

Karin's assistant, Luanne, built a special "Small Business Madness Day" email address where sales reps could send their stories and pictures. If a sales rep asked a customer where they worked and it led to a sale, they would email Luanne a celebratory photo of the rep and the new business customer or of all the new phones lined up in the back of the store transferring over data from their competitor's old phone. Every few hours, Luanne would take the success stories and pictures and compile them into a celebratory flyer she emailed out to all the stores—proving that asking the question led to sales.

Total sales quadrupled that day. The behavior worked, not only to increase sales but to inspire hope. The next morning, Karin and the DMs brought all the managers together for a region-wide conference call. The main message for this meeting was, "If focusing on small business could work for a random Tuesday, it would likely work on other days too." With the new insights from getting curious, it was time to shift focus back to the Clarity phase of the Courageous Culture Cycle.

Galvanize the Genius

Now that they knew selling to small businesses was a keeper strategy, it was vital to Galvanize the Genius—which you'll learn about in Chapter 11—by ensuring everyone understood unequivocally that selling to the small business space was their number one strategic priority.

They held rallies to explain the market opportunity and trained reps in the benefits of the plans for business customers. They asked the training team to build a "meeting in a box" filled with tips and techniques that store managers could deliver at staff meetings. The reporting team changed the scorecards to reflect the new small business targets. The small business strategy and results became a standard item in every operations review the district managers had with Karin's boss, the regional president. And they aligned the infrastructure, as we'll discuss in Chapter 12, by incorporating small business sales objectives into their quarterly compensation plans and increased the focus in new hire training.

> "It was the extreme focus and relentless execution, celebration, and accountability every single day that finally convinced the skeptics that this wasn't going away—and that this was how our team would win."
> —PETE, District Manager

The Clarity-Curiosity dance doesn't stop after one round. Once they'd established Clarity and followed through with the new sales strategy, it was time for Karin and her team to dance with Curiosity once again.

Practice the Principle

At this point, the team was making consistent progress with most of the sales reps. How could they continue the momentum? The answer came as they looked for ways to enhance the strategy, using a process called Practice the Principle (more in Chapter 10), by encouraging each district to get creative on the best approaches for their market. Each district manager team was challenged to work with their small business change agent to uncover best practices and try a unique approach to small business sales that would work best for the customer base. This is where the magic really happened.

In Cedar Bluff, Virginia, the rural store was located in a converted log cabin. Their customers were mostly contractors and farmers. This store team decided to turn their loft into a small business center, inviting customers to come in for special consultations and appointments. In this rural southern community, the small-business owners liked the personal touch and felt respected and valued in the business center.

Though located in the same state, the store in Virginia Beach, Virginia, faced different challenges stemming from seasonal dips in traffic. During the summer, beachgoing tourists flooded the store, but during the off-season there was little foot traffic. This store decided to build a makeshift "call center" in the back of the store, where store reps would proactively reach out to local small businesses to tell them about the great new plans.

The "call center" was simply the sales reps sitting around the break room table in the back of the store making outbound calls from their own cell phones. Since this was also the slow season for other businesses in the area, the owners had time to chat, and many accepted the sales rep's offer to swing by the store for an appointment and free consultation to see if they were on the most effective plan.

A third store, in Washington, DC, had local small businesses who were more likely to be law firms and lobbyists than construction workers. These customers preferred environments that felt more like a business-to-business setting than a consumer retail store. The DC team came up with the idea to give each sales rep a stipend to spend on professional clothes. Rather than the colored polo shirts or T-shirts their colleagues wore, these sales reps came to work in suits, sport coats, and dresses.

These market-by-market enhancements increased sales in each location. The local focus empowered sales reps to think strategically about what would work best in their markets—something they could do after they had mastered the fundamentals of the Clarity phase. Ultimately, the team transformed from despondency to an energized powerhouse. They were selling again and they believed in themselves—all without selling the iPhone.

That's how a Courageous Culture driven by the dance between Clarity and Curiosity transformed results for one regional sales team. The same process will work for you. In the next chapters we will give you the tools to engage the power of Clarity and Curiosity to build your Courageous Culture. First, we encourage you to continue to work through your First Tracks by identifying a strategic area to focus your team's innovation and problem solving.

FIRST TRACKS

Own the UGLY

By now you may know exactly where you want to focus your team's best thinking and innovation, and you're ready to move on to Chapter 7 where you'll work on building and communicating your vision for a Courageous Culture. But if you aren't quite sure where to start, or you need help prioritizing your focus, start with our Own the UGLY exercise.

OBJECTIVE:
To identify a strategic priority to focus your initial Courageous Cultures work.

TIME REQUIRED:
About an hour depending on depth of discussion.

PROCESS:
Own the UGLY is a series of four provocative questions to brainstorm with your team: What are we Underestimating? What's got to Go? Where are we Losing? And where are we missing the Yes?

You can do this exercise as a team or break into subgroups and have each group take a letter and work on the related questions to then read out to the team.

U—What are we Underestimating?

Competitive pressures? New technology? Risk? The opportunity that we "don't have time for"?

G—What's got to Go?

What are we doing now that doesn't make sense anymore? What processes are more habit than value? What meetings are wasting our time? What's got to go for us to be remarkable?

L—Where are we Losing?

Where are we still underperforming despite our best efforts? Why? Who's doing it better? How?

Y—Where are we missing the Yes?

What new opportunities are yearning for our attention? Where must we invest more deeply?

This Own the UGLY exercise is a quick way to clarify your focus and pick a good starting point as you incubate your Courageous Culture. Once you've answered these questions, talk with your team about one area of your business where you need your employees' best thinking and new ideas. In the next chapter, we'll talk more about how to ensure everyone has a shared understanding of what matters most, your strategic goals, and how to participate in your culture.

CHAPTER 7

Create Clarity

You've got to think about big things while you're doing small
things, so that all the small things go in the right direction.

—ALVIN TOFFLER, Author of *Future Shock*[1]

Y ou wouldn't have known he was going there. There was no
preworkshop to help him Navigate the Narrative. We were
facilitating a leadership panel at an executive off-site conference
when George, a financial services operations director, asked for the
microphone. Here's the story he shared with all of us:

I served in Afghanistan. One day we were driving through the
desert in two Humvees. I was a passenger in the lead vehicle,
and the other was close behind. I noticed that our driver was
driving very fast and it didn't feel right. I was getting more
and more nervous. I've been trained. I knew how dangerous
this was. But I didn't want to be seen as a back-seat driver, so
I kept the feedback to myself. Finally, I took out my GPS and
tracked our speed. We were going seventy-five miles an hour
on those damaged streets! It was too fast for the conditions,
but I still didn't say anything. Then, my buddy looked back
and we realized that the second Humvee was no longer behind us.

We turned back, and sure enough it had flipped. We lost a man that day. I'm haunted by the fact that I could have saved his life if I had just spoken up.

Then he continued.

The stuff we're talking about today is real. The concern you're sitting on might not be life or death, but it matters. We need to care enough to tell one another the truth—and we don't always do that. We have to figure out how to do this well. Today is an important start. I look forward to hearing your ideas.

George was off to a powerful start with a clear message: "Your concern matters. We need to care enough to speak the truth." That's Clarity. Hopefully you don't have a story like George. Thank goodness, we don't either. But you do have stories that matter, and your team needs to hear them. You found them in your initial First Tracks in Chapter 5. If you missed this step, we invite you to slow down and revisit that exercise.

When you Create Clarity, you build a foundation that gives your people safety, confidence, and direction. Once you've clarified your values and found your best story to help express your "why," you're ready to engage your team and provide that foundation. You don't have to know everything at this point, but to get started you will need Clarity about what your values look like in practice, why they're important, the most important strategic priorities, and what your people can do next.

ANSWER THEIR QUESTIONS

When you start talking about a Courageous Culture, most employees will have four big questions on their minds.

1. What do you actually mean?

They want to know how this will look in their day-to-day world. Whether you hear this question or not, these are the thoughts people have as they wonder exactly what you're talking about:

- When you say you want us to be Customer Advocates, can you give me some real examples?
- How will I know what's safe and when I've gone too far?
- When you tell me you want my innovative ideas—what kinds of ideas? How do I ensure I'm not wasting time on ideas that don't matter or won't get funded? What kinds of problems should we focus on solving?
- How do I position my ideas in a way that will be heard?
- And, oh by the way, are you sure my boss is on board? Because he's the most risk-adverse micromanager I've ever worked for. What are you going to do about people like him?
- And if you really want me to be courageous, how do I speak up when everything you've laid out here isn't working—how do I do that without being labeled as negative?

2. Why does it matter?

For many employees, this will all sound like a lot of extra work, so they need to understand why the Courageous Culture you described is better—for everyone. Be sure what you are describing is true. We once heard an executive tell his team he needed their best thinking "because we're in the fight of our lives," meaning a competitor was breathing down their necks and the company's stock price was in jeopardy. We happened to know that several people in that room really were in a "fight of their lives" with a sick family member, a kid on drugs, an aging parent for whom they had to make tough choices, and other major life challenges. His tone-deaf remark was lost on them, as they nodded politely and went back to doing their work the way they had always done it—his "why" had backfired.

3. Can I trust you?

Your team won't be able to hear anything you say about courage and innovation without first watching what you do—very closely—to see if what you do matches up with what you've said. They also want to see if you pay attention to what others do. The work you do in your First Tracks will make a difference. Are you leaving a trail that feels safe and easy to follow? Are you watching for hazards and removing obstacles? The most important work you will do in these early stages is to define your values and to Navigate the Narrative around courage and fear (Chapter 5).

4. What is expected of me?

The only way to shift a culture is to change behaviors. As you know from any shift you've made in your own life, it comes down to one behavior at a time. You can decide you want to be an Ironman triathlete, but if you've never run a 5K, you start by lacing up your shoes and going for a short run. If, on your first weekend, you tried to take swimming lessons to improve your stroke, weight training to build endurance, and ride your bike over Vail Pass, you'd end up discouraged, sore, and not much fun to be around.

Unless you are in the wonderful, unique position of building a culture from scratch, as in a few of the fast-growing start-ups we've had a chance to work with, there's probably no reason to announce "We're building a Courageous Culture!" We encourage you to read this book with your team and visualize what success looks like. We'll give you a way to do that in the First Tracks section at the close of this chapter. Then, pick one set of behaviors and work on those first. What would make the biggest difference for your organization—more problem solving, more innovative ideas, or having your team more focused on advocating for the customers?

George picked one place to start. "We need to care enough to tell one another the truth." Sure, he wanted great ideas, for teams to share best practices across geographies, and more strategic problem solving, but he knew that for his team, what came first was the courage to speak up when something isn't right.

HOW TO GET EVERYONE ALIGNED AND FOCUSED ON WHAT MATTERS MOST

Innovation starts with information. If you want your team to solve more problems or to bring more ideas, they need Clarity about where you're headed and what matters most. They need to know the one to three big strategic priorities where their ideas would make the most difference and which kinds of best practices are most important to share. And if you want them to act as Customer Advocates, they need to understand what that means in terms of specific behaviors, and how they would know if they've gone too far.

Clarify the Focus

Often, when we dig underneath the surface of organizations where leaders are frustrated at the lack of innovation or problem solving, we find that employees are totally overwhelmed with multiple priorities. Everything feels urgent and important. When their manager asks them for ideas, they don't know where to start, so they don't contribute.

Clarity of values, processes, and goals gives people the foundation to readily innovate and solve problems.[2] Tamara Ghandour, the founder of global innovation firm LaunchStreet and creator of the Innovation Quotient Edge, is an advocate for the power of starting with a clear focus on where you need innovation. In a conversation with Tamara, she explained:

> Having a clear strategic focus won't give you all the answers, but it will put you on the right path to innovation. Without it

you are trying to get up that mountain without any path. You have a lot of options to choose from, no idea which direction will get you there, and an increased sense of frustration as you step the wrong way. Clarity is that clearly defined path from which you move forward with deliberate curiosity and guidance. The innovation you discover on that path is meaningful and lasting.

Let's get back to the financial services conference where George got the team's attention about the importance of telling one another the truth through his powerful story. Each senior leader left that meeting with a clear expectation that they would meet with their teams to ensure everyone understood the three biggest strategic priorities, why they were important, and then to engage in creative problem solving to identify specific actions and behaviors for fast progress.

Check for Understanding

Mary, a dynamic vice president, did exactly that. She was one of the first to bring her managers together as a follow-up to that meeting. She kicked off the meeting with a highly motivating and inspirational message. She told a great story and worked hard to explain the "why" behind what they were doing. Most important, she translated the priorities into what they meant for the managers, and how they needed to change specific behaviors.

But as we looked around the room, we noticed that not a single person had taken notes. They were all just smiling back at her politely. We had a hunch that no one had truly picked up what she was putting down. As she handed us the microphone to begin our facilitation, we asked, "Who can tell us about one of the three priorities Mary talked about?"

You could hear the crickets. Mary's eyes opened in dismay. She had worked so hard on her presentation, but as things stood, it wasn't going to change behavior or lay the foundation to generate ideas. When it comes to Clarity, consistent communication is only half of the work. The other half is engagement—you've got to ensure your team gets it. (You'll get more tools to help with this in Chapter 11: Galvanize the Genius.)

When Mary's team couldn't tell us any of the most important priorities, it wasn't because the managers weren't listening. They were. It wasn't because they didn't care. They did. But the presentation style felt like watching TV—it was essentially passive. The change in direction was new, and the managers needed a minute to catch up and interact with what they'd heard.

Mary needed engagement through a recap and a feedback loop. We call this communication feedback loop a "check for understanding." We asked Mary to recap the three priorities, which she did slowly and deliberately. And then we asked again.

This time every manager could share all three priorities. They nailed it. An hour into the facilitation, we asked again. "What were the three priorities Mary shared?" They nailed it again. Progress. Just adding that one subtle shift, getting the team to share back what they heard, made all the difference.

It's easy to assume your team will get it the first time. After all, they're smart. They care. And, if you do say so yourself, you've crafted a careful and powerful leadership message. But the truth is, they're just catching up. You've been sitting in the planning meetings. You understand the nuance and the backstory. You wordsmithed the talking points. But for them, here it comes, all at once. It's likely that they're processing the first priority and what it means to them, while also looking at the customer-service crisis blowing up their phone and thinking about how they had only one slice of lunchmeat for little Bobby's lunch that morning and wondering if he's going to notice.

When you check for understanding, it's important to know that people got it, but it's also important to see how they're feeling. Karin learned this early in her management career from an astute boss named Ray. Karin was always extra enthusiastic at the end of her meetings. "Thanks, everyone, you've done such a great job on this plan! I know it's going to be great—now let's go do it!"

But the truth is, her over-the-top optimism was a huge source of FOSU for her team. No one wanted to be the naysayer amid all that cheerleading. Ray took her aside and suggested, "Karin, instead of concluding your meetings by telling everyone how great things are going to be, what if, instead, you asked, 'How's everyone feeling?'"

That shift was a soft invitation for her team to tell her the truth about their concerns. When she tried it, Karin started to hear legitimate concerns like: "Well, I'm worried that IT won't have the bandwidth to pull this off with everything else they have on their plates." Or, "It's a great idea, but so were your last twenty-seven ideas; which do you want us to do first?"

A good check for understanding creates engagement, ensures everyone is on the same page, and raises issues that could otherwise go unspoken. Your people can't innovate or solve problems without the certainty that they're working on and thinking about the right ideas.

In summary, as you consider how to make the shift toward a more Courageous Culture, start with Clarity about where you're headed: values, behaviors, and goals. What values will guide behavior? What behaviors are critical for success? Clarify the strategic areas where your team should focus their best thinking. Remember, information drives innovation.

FIRST TRACKS

Building a Courageous Cultures Vision

Now it's your turn to define what a Courageous Culture looks like for your organization and prioritize which behaviors you will work on first. Gather your direct report team and complete this visioning exercise. After this process, you will have a clear vision of what it means to have an organization where everyone is a Microinnovator, Problem Solver, or Customer Advocate and one specific behavior to implement.

OBJECTIVES:
- Identify a specific vision for the Courageous Culture you want to build.
- You and your team will commit to at least one behavior to start with that will help you practice and generate momentum.

TIME REQUIRED:
About two hours.

PROCESS:
1. Identify the focus areas of a Courageous Culture you want to create: microinnovation, problem solving, or customer advocacy. For example, you may be all about problem solving and innovation but are not quite ready for the customer-advocacy piece. Or it could be the opposite. Perhaps your sole focus is to improve your customer experience and you want to start with a deep focus on what it means to be a Customer Advocate. You might want to start more narrowly and focus your team on solving customer-impacting issues or how to get more creative at solving customer problems on the spot. Or, like George, you may want to start with a focus on problem solving by speaking truth respectfully.

2. Take the focus you identified in step one and create a focus question. Here are a few examples:
   - Imagine it's two years from now and we have microinnovation happening at every level of the organization. What behaviors are we seeing at the executive, manager, and frontline level?

- What would it really mean for us to have an organization in which every employee was empowered and encouraged to be a true Customer Advocate? What behaviors would we see at the executive, manager, and frontline level?
- How do we get better at solving the most important problems impacting our business? What behaviors do we need to develop, encourage, and reward at the executive, manager, and frontline level?

Notice that every one of these questions is focused on identifying behaviors. That's vital to make this vision something you can clearly describe, train to, reinforce, observe, and measure. One way to ensure the conversation you are about to have is focused on behaviors is to imagine if you could hire a videographer to record what was happening on a day two years from now. What behaviors would she capture when your vision is a reality?

3. Give every member of your direct report team three stacks of sticky notes, each stack a different color. The colors represent one of three levels of the organization: executive, manager, and frontline. Share your focus question with the team and ask all of them to silently brainstorm the related behaviors they would see at each level of the organization when that vision is achieved. Ask them to write one behavior per sticky note and make a pile of behaviors for each level. At the end of this step, each person will have three piles of sticky notes. Note: it might be tempting to do this as a group discussion, but doing the introverted work first ensures every member of your team contributes her best thinking and allows the ideas to stand on their own merit.

Example behaviors might include:

Executive
We constantly talk to customers to understand their perspective.
We celebrate innovation at every level.

We train our employees on how to solve problems and think critically.

Manager
We ensure all employees understand our strategic priorities and
*   where we need their best thinking to improve the business.*
We start every team meeting with a courageous question.
We share best practices with our peers.

Frontline
We speak up when we see a problem.
We constantly ask, "How can we do this better?"
We find creative solutions to delight our customers.

4. Identify three separate areas (one area for each level) where team members will place their sticky notes. Have team members randomly place there notes in the designated areas.

5. After all the sticky notes have been placed in each area, ask the team to review what everyone wrote. Once they've read through all the notes, have them rearrange the notes in clusters of similar behaviors or themes. Then ask them to identify the one clustered theme in each level that they believe would make the biggest difference in achieving the target vision.

6. As a team, discuss the prioritized clusters. What themes emerged? Are there consistent priorities across the organization or do they differ by level? Conclude the discussion by working with the team to identify one (maximum of two) behaviors for each level that will serve as your starting point.

7. As a team, commit to the behaviors you identified for your level. How will you implement it? Schedule a time in thirty days when you will review your progress.

CHAPTER 8

Cultivate Curiosity

We're not just paying people to work—we're paying them for
their innovative, wonderful, world-changing ideas.
—LESLI WARD, Vice President Human Resources,
UF Health Jacksonville

aura, an IT vice president at a midsized energy company, was
excited to spend some time with her teams, hold a few skip-level
meetings with her direct-reports' teams, and see their new
system in action. Her team had been holding calls every week to
discuss the users' experiences, and all the feedback had been positive.
She hoped to collect some great stories to share with the CEO about
how the new system was making things easier for the customer
service reps and, ultimately, for their customers.

Before her first meeting, Laura sat down with a customer service
rep and asked, "Can you show me your favorite part of the new
system?"

The rep attempted to pull up the first screen. But after five minutes they were both still staring at an hourglass and waiting for the
page to load. The rep looked apologetically at Laura and said, "I'm
sorry to waste your time. This usually takes a while."

Laura's jaw dropped. The vendor had promised the new system
would be seven times faster—not slower. "Can you show me another page?" she asked.

She sat through another slow load time. She turned to the rep. "Is it always like this?"

"Oh, yeah. We're used to it at this point, but the system has some other nice features."

Laura thanked the rep and hurried to a quiet conference room where she could call her team. After ten minutes of testing, they realized that the center's servers didn't have the capacity to run the new system. Hundreds of reps had been suffering through a ridiculous wait that wasted their and their customers' time.

Week after week, supervisors had sat in on user-experience calls, fully aware of the issue, and hadn't said a word. No one had ever raised the issue.

After replacing the server and ensuring everything was back on track, Laura went back to the reps on the user experience team and asked why they had never brought this up.

> Well, no one ever asked us about the speed. Our boss told us that we needed to be "change agents" and model excitement for the new system—no matter what. Under no circumstances were we to be negative. So we just smiled, sucked it up, and dealt with it.

We opened *Courageous Cultures* with an assortment of quotes from frustrated executives who, like Laura, were perplexed at seemingly easy situations that didn't work—even when everyone involved was reasonably competent and cared. These cultures were characterized by safe silence. In the previous chapter you established a baseline of Clarity. The next step to shift the culture from silence to consistent contribution is to Cultivate Curiosity.

Cultivate Curiosity means to intentionally seek out ideas, engagement, and solutions. In organizations with a strong Curiosity culture, executives ensure that infrastructure and training encourage microinnovation, sharing ideas, and advocating for customers. Leaders at every level ask courageous questions to uncover new

ideas, and employees consistently look for ways to make things better—and then share their discoveries.

Laura's situation is far too common. The "no one asked" reply
might be frustrating, but it is one of the most frequent obstacles to
a Courageous Culture. Recall the leading reasons people don't share
ideas:

1. People don't think leadership wants their ideas.
2. No one asks.
3. They lack confidence to share.
4. They lack the skills to share effectively.
5. People don't think anything will happen, so they don't bother.

It becomes obvious that asking can help overcome these challenges (number two most obviously). As an engineering design
manager shared with us, "When people don't share, they're probably afraid or they just don't know how to get there. They don't feel
like they have a good execution plan or know if their idea is even
something we could do." When people are asked regularly and see
a response, they feel valued for their ideas and gain the confidence
to share.

HOW TO CULTIVATE CURIOSITY

Cultivating Curiosity isn't simply a matter of asking more questions. That helps, but it's not just that you ask. In Courageous Cultures, leaders ask regularly and skillfully. You ask in ways that draw
out people's best thinking, new ideas, and customer-focused solutions. Everyone knows that when you ask, you sincerely want to
know and are committed to taking action on what you learn. Three
qualities distinguish how leaders ask questions in a Courageous
Culture: they are intentional, vulnerable, and action focused.

Intentional

Cultivating Curiosity starts with intention: you must ask—a lot. Your leaders have to ask more than might seem reasonable. This kind of asking goes way beyond an open-door policy. In fact, most open-door policies are a passive leadership cop-out. "I'm approachable. I have an open door" puts the responsibility on the team, not the leader. That's a problem because most of the ideas you need will never walk through your open door. There's too much friction to overcome: time away from their normal work, not knowing how their manager will respond, or not even realizing they have an idea to share. John Dore, senior executive program director at the London Business School, explains that permission isn't enough. "Don't permit innovation, expect it. Whenever we hear something is 'allowed' or 'OK' human beings have a natural tendency to become sheepish."[1] To overcome these hesitations, ask with intention and build systems that make sharing the norm.

Vulnerable

Have you ever watched a leader ask for feedback and then defensively justify their decisions and shoot down objections? We have too. In fact, we've done it ourselves. As Lorenzo, a talented manager, told David early in his first senior leadership role, "You asked for my perspective and now you're telling me all the reasons it's wrong. Why should I waste my time?" Cultivating Curiosity requires leaders to approach their work with confidence and humility. If you're not vulnerable enough to admit that you can grow, that the current situation can improve, or that there might be a better way, you'll never get the ideas you need.

Action Focused

We've sat through strategic planning sessions and focus groups during which leaders asked questions and everyone in the room knew that the answers didn't matter. Sometimes, even when the leaders had good intentions, they lacked the ability or willingness to act on what they heard. That's one reason that mastering the Clarity phase of the Courageous Cultures Cycle is vital: you gain credibility with your team that you can make good ideas work. To Cultivate Curiosity, people need to know that you will act on what you learn. Action takes many forms. It might be that you implement the idea, that the feedback informs your decision, that you take it all in and then respond with next steps, or maybe it's simply releasing the team to take action on their ideas.

BEST PRACTICES TO FIND THE BEST IDEAS

When we looked at the kinds of questions that are intentional, vulnerable, and focused on action, a theme emerged: the questions themselves were courageous. They were very different from the generic improvement questions that average leaders ask. We've called these courageous questions and they are your number one way to Cultivate Curiosity.

Courageous Questions

Courageous questions address the concerns your people have about whether you want to hear what they're thinking and whether you have the confidence and competence to do something with the answer. A courageous question differs from a generic "How can we be better?" question in three ways. When you ask a courageous question, you:

1. **Get Specific.** First, a courageous question focuses on a specific activity, behavior, or outcome. This is a critical behavior to Cultivate Curiosity: ask for what you need. We will occasionally hear from leaders who complain about the quality of ideas or how so many ideas aren't relevant to their most

important strategic priorities. The answer is straightforward: ask for what you need.

For example, rather than ask, "How can we improve?" ask, "What is the number one frustration of our largest customer? What's your analysis? What would happen if we solved this? How can we solve it?" Or, "For the next two quarters our most important priority is customer retention. We need every idea we can get to help keep our best customers. What is the number one reason you see customers leave? What's the greatest obstacle to keeping our best customers? What's the number one low-cost action we can take to improve our customer's experience?"

2. **Be Humble.** Next, a courageous question creates powerful vulnerability. When you ask any of these sample questions, you are implicitly saying, "I know I'm not perfect. I know I can improve." This is a strong message—if you sincerely mean it.

You send the message that you are growing and want to improve. This, in turn, gives your team permission to grow and be in process themselves. It also makes it safe to share real feedback. When you say, "What is the greatest obstacle?" you acknowledge that there is an obstacle and you want to hear about it.

Humility is at the heart of the question Don Yager, chief operating officer of Mural Corporation, likes to consistently ask his frontline team: "What are our policies that suck?" That humble question quickly identifies anything that's getting in the way of a great customer experience.

3. **Don't Respond—Yet.** Finally, courageous questions require the asker to listen without defensiveness. This is where well-intentioned leaders often get into trouble. They ask a good question, but they weren't prepared to hear feedback that made them uncomfortable or challenged their pet project. They leap to explain or defend.

Asking for feedback and ignoring it is worse than not asking at all. When you ask a courageous question, allow yourself to take in the feedback. Take notes, thank everyone for taking the time and having the confidence to share their perspective. With many courageous questions, you'll get conflicting perspectives. That's okay. Describe the next steps. If you need to process and then respond, tell them when that will happen.

Courageous questions are the workhorses for leaders who are serious about Cultivating Curiosity. Check out the sidebar for examples of courageous questions that will get you started.

COURAGEOUS QUESTIONS

- What is the problem we have that no one talks about?
- What do we do that really annoys our customers?
- What is the greatest obstacle to your productivity?
- What must I do better as a leader if we are to be successful?
- What do you think we could do differently next time to help this project (or person) succeed?
- What recommendations do you have before we start on this conversion?
- What are you most afraid of with this program/project/process?
- What is the biggest source of conflict you're having working with X department? (How might we be contributing to the issue?)
- What's sabotaging our success?

How Can We?

One of the most powerful courageous questions to Cultivate Curiosity starts with only three words. When your team is stuck between conflicting goals or constraints, the question that will help them get unstuck and generate ideas is, "How can we?" This question starts with the confidence that your team can succeed. We can do this. But it also includes the humility to recognize you don't have the answer yet. We can do this—but it will take all of us to figure it out.

When you ask "How can we?" it's often useful to follow up with finding the *and* between two seemingly disconnected or opposing goals. "How can we" works because it focuses your team on solutions. Rather than focus on roadblocks, obstacles, and constraints, you've guided the team to look for what's possible. That's a totally different energy and will help even your most stodgy team members to move from objections to solutions.

Time

In our conversation with Jason Fried, cofounder of Basecamp, he observed that leaders who are frustrated when people don't creatively solve problems should pay attention to workload. Creative problem solving, he said, "requires time to think, consider, and marinade. In most companies, there's no time for that. Calendars are chock full and leaders don't understand that they've spread people too thin." There are no easy answers to how you can build in margin for reflection, but to start making this shift, consider how you would react if you encountered a productive team member standing at the window, staring into space. You ask, "Hey, what are you up to?" and they reply, "Thinking."

CREATIVE WAYS TO CULTIVATE CURIOSITY

Throughout our research, we discovered several fantastic methods leaders used to draw out people's best thinking, new ideas, and customer-focused solutions. We've included some of our favorites here. We're certain that one or more of them will work for you or spark a creative way to bring out the best ideas in your organization. (We'd love to hear from you if you've got a fun, creative, or effective way to Cultivate Curiosity in your organization. You can reach us at info@LetsGrowLeaders.com.)

At the Touch of a Button

Nate Brown, cofounder of CX Accelerator, gave every member of his frontline team a "CX magic button" for their desks. The button plugs into the computer via USB. When an employee has an idea on how to improve the customer experience, she physically hits the button and a form opens immediately on her computer where she can easily record her idea or customer feedback. The button serves as a constant reminder to be a Customer Advocate, plus it feels easy and fun. Nate then takes the themes he hears and digs deeper when he's out talking to the team.

Jon King, vice president of operations at TaskUs, a fast-growing, tech-enabled business services company, created an AskJon email, solely for ideas of innovation and community building—creating a consistent flow of great ideas, including a food pantry for any of their families in need. Jon said, "The amount of trust and respect fostered from this one program has been immense."

The Patient Perspective

Jill K. Herr, a director of clinical operations in rehabilitation at Well-Span Health, shared this best practice:

> We assign one team member to speak for the patient in a pertinent meeting. When it's a team member's turn to attend the meeting as a patient, they don't weigh in from their usual perspective during that time. They focus on thinking and speaking like a patient. If it's your turn to represent the patient, that's all you do. Your entire job as we are making decisions that will affect the patients' experience is to consider, "As a patient, what would I want/say?"

We used this most when we were building our electronic documentation system. So, for example, in our acute-care environment, we were working on a scheduling system so departments wouldn't show up at the same time to see a patient. Rehab would know when the patient was getting a test, in imaging, or being seen by a respiratory therapist. This is important, because in the past, we could show up to provide physical therapy and find an empty room.

During this discussion, the "patient" raised his hand and said, "I want to know my schedule as well. I want to know when my doctor is coming to see me. My family wants to know what time my therapy is so they can be here to be involved." What resulted is "transparent scheduling"—still a work in process but making a huge impact.

Workaround Workouts

We were facilitating an executive off-site meeting working through standardizing procedures when Josh, the vice president, said, "Can I just be real for a minute? How many of your teams have serious workarounds in place to get this done?"

Every executive in the room reluctantly raised their hand.

He continued:

How do we know if these are great ideas that everyone should be doing or sloppy practices that will bite us down the road? Some of these workarounds are probably game-changing ideas that would benefit everyone. And I'm sure there are some that we would all cringe if we knew they were going on. We need to get a handle on what's really happening. What if we had a workaround workout week where everyone can share how they're really getting the work done? We promise amnesty if they're not following protocol—no one will get in trouble. That way we can be sure they will tell us the truth. We can find the good ideas and best practices and figure out how to make them work for everyone else, buckle down on the workarounds that will get us into trouble, and explain why they're not viable solutions.

And so, the concept of the workaround workout was born. A week of amnesty to demonstrate nonstandard approaches can help you find and solve inefficiencies as well as identify and scale improvements created by the people closest to the work.

Team Masterminds

Molly, a director at a tech giant, creates an opportunity for her team to crowdsource ideas through team mastermind sessions. All team members bring a strategic business challenge they're wrestling with and pitch it to the group for ideas. They all get an opportunity to share a challenge and explain why it's hard, what they've tried, and where they need some ideas. Once they've explained the challenge, the other team members ask probing questions and share their best ideas.

Crowdsourcing

We've come across several approaches that facilitate employees sharing and collaborating on ideas. In a conversation with Carlos, a director at a large financial services company, he described his company's online system to crowdsource and vet ideas. Employees share their ideas, microinnovations, or best practices in an online form. The system immediately routes the idea to their supervisor, who does a quick review. If the idea passes basic criteria, the supervisor shares it and opens it up for "likes." Other employees can then endorse the idea with a thumbs-up, just like on social media platforms—and the most popular solutions rise to the top for further exploration and vetting.

Open Boards

Several of the leaders we talked with had some form of a white-board system where employees could write their ideas on the wall. This represents a low-tech solution for smaller teams or where technical crowdsourcing isn't available. Colleagues could contribute additional thoughts as they went about their day.

Bring-a-Friend Meetings

It's tempting to think we must have it all figured out before wasting our team's time when raising new strategic issues or concerns. We've also seen leaders struggle to promote people who haven't fully developed their problem-solving and strategic-thinking skills. But if you're really working to build people's leadership capacity and Cultivate Curiosity, it's also important to sometimes bring your folks in before you (or they) have a clue. Let them see you wrestle in the muck. Get their input too. "We could do this . . . but there's that and that to consider . . . and also the other thing." One easy way to do this is through "Bring-a-Friend" staff meetings—a technique Karin learned early in her career from one of her favorite bosses, Maureen. Once in a while, invite your direct reports to bring one of their high-potential employees along to your staff meeting. Of course, avoid anything supersensitive but be as transparent as possible.

Curiosity Tours

The goal behind a Curiosity Tour is to build trust and energize your team while learning what happens and how things actually work. A Curiosity Tour is like management by walking around, but with a limited focus. Your only job is to show up with Curiosity. As you observe your people, ask:

- Why are employees using this that way?
- How are customers responding?
- What seems difficult here?
- What's working differently (better or worse) than I expected?
- What can the team teach you that you didn't know?

These best practices to Cultivate Curiosity have several features in common. First, they make sharing ideas routine. It's not unusual. It doesn't take extra effort. It's expected. Next, there is a system supporting the ask. Whether it's the magic button, the crowdsourced feedback platform, identifying a team member to play a role, or even a plain whiteboard, there's infrastructure to support the ask.

Finally, they make speaking up visible. There's a big difference between a team member playing the role of a patient saying "I want to know my schedule" in a team meeting and that same team member visiting her manager to share the same thought. You can see your neighbor hit that magic button. When you crowdsource feedback, everyone sees what's shared. Visibly sharing ideas normalizes the behavior and gives everyone a chance to respond and incorporate the idea.

OVERCOMING SAFE SILENCE

Even with the best systems in place and leaders committed to asking courageous questions, sometimes it takes more to draw out your team's best ideas. First, you've got to make it safe. Your team has questions of their own: Do you really want to hear what I have to say? Is it safe to share a critical view or a perspective different from yours? Are you humble enough to hear my feedback? Are you confident and competent enough to do something with what you hear?

Then there's the scar tissue to consider. Chances are that even if you're the most receptive leader employees have ever worked for, some manager in the past has squashed a great idea or even retaliated against them for speaking up. Often when we hear stories that start with "the last time I shared an idea I got in trouble," that last time was from the distant past. If you want to free their best ideas from the prison of safety, you need to address these concerns. Ultimately, you want a space where ideas flow freely and speaking up is the norm. But what if you're not there yet? If you sense that your team is reluctant to share ideas or speak the truth, start by building in as much visible anonymity to the process as possible.

Visible anonymity means everyone knows that everyone else is contributing, but they don't know who said what. This makes contributing feel normal but without the risk of raising what could be an unpopular idea. Contrast that with this anonymous sharing we discovered in one team: The manager placed a suggestion box in a back room. The only reason to go to that room was to submit a suggestion. To alleviate this problem, the manager also placed a bowl of candy near the suggestion box. Now team members might be going back for candy or to make a suggestion.

This manager is trying hard to make it safe to share ideas, but think about the message this sends. The entire system still screams "sharing ideas is risky—better to have people think you're eating candy than contributing to the well-being of our team or company."

Fear Forage

A Fear Forage is one way you can use visible anonymity to Cultivate Curiosity and surface anxiety or concerns. One of our favorite Fear Forages came when we were leading an executive off-site meeting with a group of successful senior leaders considering a strategic initiative that would require an exponential increase in collaboration across departments full of people who were geographically dispersed, who seldom worked together, and who had competing objectives. We were working through an Own the UGLY exercise (see First Tracks in Chapter 6), but we had a hunch that we weren't getting to the heart of the issue—the polite conversation was going in circles. We worried that if they didn't acknowledge and talk about that, their carefully crafted plans wouldn't stand a chance.

We gave every leader an index card to anonymously write down their hopes and fears about the project. The hopes easily fell into a few categories. They hoped the strategy would lead to increased revenue, improve the customer experience, and improve the brand. They were united in the vision of why this was important. The most interesting outcome was the universal fear. Every person in the room feared the same thing: Could the others in the room be counted on to execute this strategy well? But no one had raised the issue. We started reading the similar fears aloud. Two-thirds of the way through, everyone got the point. Yikes. If the members of the senior team were this worried about one another's ability to execute, how would they convince their teams to take those risks? Before they did anything else, they needed to get real and talk about their perceptions and concerns. This Fear Forage exercise is a fast and simple way to get the unspoken fears and concerns into the room.

Here are a few more ways you can use visible anonymity to move through safe silence:

- Do a quick two- or three-question online survey. Discuss at the next opportunity.
- Meet with the team one-on-one (so everyone knows you're talking to everyone).
- Ask a neutral person to help you get a pulse on how people feel and what they think.
- Have everyone write a key question or concern on a note card, collect the cards, redistribute them, and ask everyone to represent the question or concern on their card.

You don't want to rely on these techniques forever, but when you have a fearful team you can prime the pump as you're building trust and establishing the groundwork for how the team will work together. The tools in the next chapter will help you take what you learn in these activities and respond in ways that help your people transition from fear to a Courageous Culture.

FIRST TRACKS

Courageous Questions

OBJECTIVES:
- To check in on the behaviors your team identified in Chapter 7.
- To identify the most appropriate Cultivate Curiosity techniques to experiment with.
- To select the best courageous questions to ask and identify your plan for asking them.

TIME REQUIRED:
About an hour.

PROCESS:
In the last chapter, you worked with your team to cultivate your vision and identified a few specific behaviors you each were going to practice consistently as your starting point to building a Courageous Culture. Before you jump into the next First Tracks exercise, be sure to check in to ask about how those behaviors are working and the impact people have seen.

Assemble your direct report team and answer the following questions together:

- Where do you most need your team's best ideas? What do you need to get most curious about now?
- Which Cultivate Curiosity techniques will you use to uncover your team's best ideas?

- What courageous questions (see the sidebar earlier in the chapter) do you most need to ask your team?
- When will you commit to use one of the Cultivate Curiosity techniques or ask the courageous questions you identified?

CHAPTER 9

Respond with Regard

The most promising ideas begin from novelty and then add familiarity.

—ADAM GRANT, Author of *Originals* and *Give and Take*[1]

Melinda is a seasoned entrepreneur and fellow keynote speaker who had built a successful business from scratch. Karin met her at a conference where they were both presenting. Given her past success, what Melinda told Karin was surprising:

> I'm so intrigued by this research you're doing on FOSU and the downstream consequences for employees and organizations. The truth is, I'm one of those people. I had such a bad experience when I was twenty-three that I would never offer my opinion at work again.
>
> I was just out of college and so eager to make an impact in my new role. I had tons of ideas and was always looking for ways to make things better. So I offered my opinion on everything—which, as it turns out, was exhausting to everyone around me. I got fired and was completely devastated. After all, my heart was in the right place. I was gung ho. The truth is that I was committed, but clumsy.

Once I got back on my feet in a new job, I kept my head down, my mouth shut, and just did my job. I had this FOSU thing you talk about in a big way. And I was miserable. It's why I eventually had to go start my own business. I knew I would never speak up to an employer again.

Melinda's experience is just one example of where Courageous Cultures often break down: leaders' response (or lack of response) when people speak up with ideas, solutions, or critiques.

Recall the research findings: 50 percent of respondents said they believed that if they share an idea, it won't be taken seriously. Even more concerning is that the number one reason people said they would keep a microinnovation to themselves (56 percent) is concern that they wouldn't get credit for their idea. And then there are the 67 percent who said their leadership operates from "this is how we've always done it."

Feeling ignored because no one responded. Concern about not getting credit. Believing nothing will happen. What do these findings have in common? These aren't failures to ask—these are failures to respond and respond well. How you and leaders at every level respond to ideas and feedback will either build momentum or crush your culture before it gets started. We call this behavior Respond with Regard. Responding with regard means you receive ideas and react in ways that respect the other person, build momentum, improve your employees' strategic thinking, and generate more useful ideas. In this chapter, you'll receive practical ways to Respond with Regard and build a flow of ideas that are increasingly strategic, relevant, and useful.

WHEN RESPONSE BREAKS DOWN

In our experience, this skill is one of the most underappreciated and rarely taught in most leadership and management training. Unfortunately, that lack of training results in three common leadership failures.

Apathy

We met Nolan, an energetic and creative vice president who has repeatedly brought ideas to his CEO that would save the company millions of dollars. The CEO dismissed the ideas and replied, "Just do the job I hired you to do." Nolan is able to do that work without breaking a sweat, so, he says, "I take a long lunch every week and take flying lessons. When I get home, I work on starting my own business."

This is an example of the first mistake leaders make when re-sponding to ideas and feedback: they respond with apathy. Perhaps they take the employee's ideas as a threat to their own competence, a challenge to their authority, or they just don't want to be bothered. Regardless of the reason, when your managers respond with silence or apathy, it's a guaranteed way to kill a Courageous Culture.

Avoidance

David witnessed a classic example of the second response problem at a midsized education-focused nonprofit that was experiencing high turnover. At the board of directors' request, the CEO con-ducted an employee survey that asked courageous questions to help uncover the challenges behind the turnover and asked for potential solutions. When the survey results came in, the CEO didn't like what she read. The employees had accurately diagnosed problems with her leadership and the cadre of senior leaders who passed along her dysfunctional policies. She wasn't able to own her role in the organization's problems, so rather than respond to the feedback, she stuck it in a drawer and never addressed it with her staff. As you can imagine, after she avoided their feedback, the staff felt ignored and devalued. Their retention issues escalated.

This is an extreme example of the most common way that leaders don't Respond with Regard: avoidance. The worst form of avoidance is when you combine it with apathy. This happens most often when a leader thinks it would be a good idea to ask for feedback but hasn't committed to responding to what they hear. The feedback comes in, but it's inconvenient or unsettling, and so the leader doesn't respond to it. You're better off not to ask than to ask and not respond.

Poor Reactions to Off-Base Ideas

The third problem is more nuanced. Several executives, when they heard about our work with Courageous Cultures, told us, "Oh, that's not our issue. Our problem is these damn millennials can't stop speaking up. They complain about everything."

"And do you listen?"

"Some of the time, but after a while you can only take so much."

Which prompts the question: What happens next after you're tired and they're ignored? It's only a matter of time before they stop trying or find someplace else to work that will listen. It's worth the investment to help your team better position their ideas. Many people will start by speaking up and contributing ideas, but like Melinda, they don't do it elegantly. The third problem is responding poorly to incomplete, off-base, or inelegant ideas. Responding with Regard to these sorts of ideas makes all the difference in whether you'll get the contributions you do need next time.

HOW TO RESPOND WITH REGARD

Recently, David made a "contribution"—he donated blood through the Red Cross. What happened next is a great example of how you can Respond with Regard to get more solutions, ideas, and critical thinking from your team members. Four weeks after donating, he received the following email:

Thank you for giving blood with the American Red Cross on May 23. Your blood donation was sent to The Johns Hopkins Hospital in Baltimore, Maryland, to help a patient in need. Your donation is on its way to change lives!

Every day, patients receive blood for a variety of conditions including life-threatening illnesses, blood disorders, and traumas. Your blood donations are critical to helping save patients' lives. Schedule your next donation today!

The message was followed by a large red button to schedule his next donation. This is a fantastic example of how to Respond with Regard. There were three elements that you can include in your responses: gratitude, process, and invitation. They thanked him, told him how his contribution was making a difference, and invited him to do it again. The same approach works for leaders when team members contribute ideas.

Gratitude

If you want more solutions, start with thank you. We see many leaders overlook this easy step. When people take the time to think about how things could be better, let them know you appreciate it: "I really appreciate your taking time to think about how we can do this better. Thank you!" Celebrate solutions, yes, but also celebrate the act of contributing. Call attention to and celebrate employees who share new ideas and solutions—even when those solutions don't work. You get more of what you celebrate and encourage. Don't celebrate only the ideas that work; celebrate the act of sharing thoughtful ideas and solutions. You'll get more solutions and some of those *will* work.

Process

Next, share the process. Let them know what happened with their idea and the relevant time frame. You may not have an elegant automated response system like the Red Cross, but it only takes a moment to circle back and close the loop with team members. If it will take six months before you consider these ideas because of other strategic priorities, say so and explain the other priorities (your employees may surprise you with ideas that achieve those objectives).

Invitation

Finally, invite them to do it again—to think, problem solve, and advocate for your customer. The Red Cross invited David with a large red button to schedule his next contribution. Your invitation to contribute again can take many forms. If their ideas need work, give them the additional information they need and ask them to recraft it. If their ideas were tried in the past and didn't work, tell them what you learned from that attempt and ask them to consider how to overcome those problems. Even if you can't use the ideas at all, a sincere "I'd love to hear your thoughts about how we can achieve our goal this year" will keep the ideas flowing.

FOUR WAYS TO RESPOND TO AN IDEA

When managers struggle to respond elegantly to the ideas they receive, it's often because they feel overwhelmed. To simplify things a bit, let's look at the four types of ideas they are likely to hear. These four categories can help your managers to respond in ways that generate more critical thinking, microinnovations, and solutions. When an employee speaks up with an idea or suggestion, there are four possibilities and four different responses available. When the employee's idea is:

1. Already implemented—explain where and how the idea is in use and who the team member might talk with to learn more;
2. Incomplete—what additional information can you give the team member? What questions or obstacles does she need to address? Can you ask him to resubmit his idea with the additional information thought through?
3. Ready to be trialed and tested—can you invite the team member to help with the trial?
4. Not moving forward—what considerations made the idea less valuable right now? Is there additional information that would help the employee come up with a more relevant or usable idea next time?

Responding with Regard isn't difficult, but it does require your leaders to focus on the bigger picture and long-term outcomes. Sometimes this means finding small wins that might not be game changers today but create long-term potential. We met Damon, a senior leader in health care, who shared what became one of our favorite ways to Respond with Regard. Damon had served in the military before his career in health care and learned this strategy from one of his commanding officers. "When someone speaks up with an idea, find a yes. You may not be able to implement the entire idea, and the piece you say yes to may not be transformative or worth a huge effort—it might even be a small headache. But when you can say yes to something, it brings down the walls."

What a powerful way to think about how you respond to ideas! Damon smiled as he shared this strategy. "When my commanding officer first gave me this advice, I laughed at it. But now I use it nearly every day. If you can find a small win for them, meet them where they are, it changes their outlook and, in many cases, they'll run through walls for you."

Find the yes is another example of gratitude, process, and invitation—wrapped up into one straightforward response. People feel seen, appreciated, and know that they make a difference. Nothing communicates that you truly want to hear ideas more than finding a yes and getting that idea into the world.

RESPONDING WHEN YOU CAN'T USE AN IDEA

There will also be times when you can't "find a yes" or use the idea. In these critical moments, you can still build momentum and cultivate teams of Microinnovators, Problem Solvers, and Customer Advocates. Again, start with gratitude. If you want people thinking more deeply, thank them for their contribution (even if it's not quite as deep as you would have liked).

Next, explain what happened. If you put their idea in a trial, sent it to a focus group, or did anything at all with it, let them know what happened. What problems did it run into? Were there competing priorities? Did the solution break down or prove impractical during testing? Take a few seconds to respond and close the loop. It will energize the person who shared their idea—even if you couldn't use it.

If the idea was off target or didn't support a strategic priority, clarify your focus. When you can't use an idea, the problem might be that they didn't have enough information to make a good suggestion. What information can you add that will help them think more deeply about the issue? Give them the information they need to think more strategically. Finally, once you've clarified the focus and given them more information, invite them to keep thinking and to share what they come up with.

RESPONDING TO PROBLEMS

Cultivating courage doesn't mean your leadership team gets distracted by every employee complaint. A British executive we interviewed said it well: "Sometimes people just need to have a good moan." Taking action whenever employees complain, vent, or "have a good moan" is fruitless and exhausting. There is an art to finding the useful ideas within a complaint. As one health care manager shared with us, "When people complain, don't dismiss it. I look for patterns and what's really causing the problem. See if there's something we can do that will fix it." An IT director shared her approach: "When someone brings me a complaint, I listen, then ask them what action would make this better? Often, they pause and say, 'No action required. Thanks for listening.'"

When you ask courageous questions, team members are likely to share problems—after all, some courageous questions explicitly ask them to reveal the problems that keep them from being effective. When you hear problems, resist the urge to jump in with a quick fix. These are great opportunities to build trust—especially if you've uncovered the problem by asking a question. One study found that when "someone says their leader always responds constructively to problems, they're about twelve times more likely to recommend the company as a great employer."[2] When you're following up a courageous question, two questions that work to build trust and invite the other person to deeper thought are: "How can I be most helpful here?" or "Do you have thoughts about the best way to solve this?"

WHAT TO DO WHEN YOU WONDER, "WHAT WERE THEY THINKING?"

We've looked at how to Respond with Regard to ideas in general, how to find a yes, and how to respond when you can't use an idea. But what do you do when you encounter something that just doesn't make sense? These moments are opportunities to improve Clarity, improve people's skills, and perhaps discover something new.

When David was a twelve-year-old Boy Scout, he found himself on the receiving end of a "what were you thinking?" moment. He and his friends were on a camping trip and had carefully planned a menu, bought groceries, but were struggling to cook breakfast. Bud, their adult leader, walked by. He stopped, looked at their frying pan, arched an eyebrow, and asked, "What are you making?"

They held up the pan of blue-green gelatinous charred mess. "Blueberry pancakes?"

David has never forgotten what Bud did next. He crouched down next to the fire with David and his friends. "Well, let's see what we have here."

The boys explained their concoction. It was autumn and blueberries weren't in season. So they'd bought the next best alternative they could find: blueberry pie filling. They'd substituted a cup of pie filling for a cup of fresh blueberries. But it doesn't work that way. The pie filling added more liquid and sugar to the batter than plain blueberries. Not knowing any better, they mixed it up, poured it in the pan, and watched it burn as they poked it with a spatula.

Bud saw what had happened, explained the problem, and asked, "So if you've got too much liquid in your batter, what do you need to do?"

He coached the boys through adding more dry ingredients until they had the right consistency. Then he helped them cook the resulting "pancake." The texture still wasn't right. They didn't make nice neat circles. And they turned a strange color—somewhere between forest green and steel gray. But the taste was heavenly! No syrup required. With Bud's help, they'd invented a new breakfast delicacy: The Slimer. David and his friends incorporated those Slimer pancakes into camping menus for years to come. When you see something that makes little sense, it's normal to feel frustrated, concerned, or even angry. Your team should know better, right? But that moment of exasperation is also an opportunity. What you heard or saw could be:

- A cool new microinnovation.
- A good idea that needs refinement.

- A lack of understanding.
- Ignorance of critical rules or process.
- They weren't thinking at all.
- Or it could just be a truly bad idea.

Regardless, these are opportunities to improve. Your people can learn. You can improve your processes. You can leverage new ideas, but it's easy to miss these opportunities if you react with frustration. If Bud had shaken his head at their slimy mess and told them to cook eggs like the other kids, they would have missed out on Slimers. To take advantage of these moments and identify the opportunity, use Bud's curiosity. Approach the team with, "Well, let's see what we have here."

A common reason people make "what were they thinking?" mistakes is lack of Clarity. They don't know where procedures are mandatory or where they should make their own decisions. Your genuine Curiosity will uncover these gaps. Now you can go back to the Clarity phase and level up your training or communication.

If you've shared the focus, checked for understanding, and someone brings you an idea that seems way off target, resist the urge to get upset. Instead, use it as an opportunity for a microcoaching session. Ask how the idea will help achieve the goal. Taking a moment to be curious can help uncover great ideas or help a team member understand what a great idea looks like. For example, "Thanks for thinking about this with us. Can you walk me through how your idea would help us achieve 100 percent on-time delivery?"

You'll get different answers to this question. Some will say, "Oh, I hadn't really thought it through." In which case you can reply, "I'd love to get your thoughts once you've had a chance to think it through."

Often, "what were they thinking?" moments reveal a new approach. Take the time to understand why they did what they did and you might just uncover the key to better customer service or employee engagement. Help them refine the idea and think about how they can share it with other teams. If they weren't thinking at all, now you know. Is this an opportunity to help your team member grow or a sign that the person is a poor fit for this role?

Sometimes, when you wonder, "What were they thinking?" it's not the idea that bothers you—it's how they shared it. This happened to Karin early in her career when she made a well-intended but clumsy move. She was an inexperienced HR manager who had been asked by her vice president to represent him at a meeting about fixing a serious attendance problem. After getting frustrated by suggestions that she knew wouldn't fix the root cause, she announced to a room full of vice presidents, all of whom had at least a decade more experience than her, that "you're completely wrong on this."

Now, in an advanced Courageous Culture, they might have invited her to explain, but in most organizations, that's a career-limiting move. Fortunately, the senior vice president took her aside after the meeting and explained the political realities of their culture:

> Karin, you've got great ideas, but you're incredibly clumsy. As a manager, you don't tell a room full of VPs in a meeting with their peers and in front of their boss that they're wrong! You quietly take notes and then talk with a few of them individually to get input and buy-in for your ideas. You really ticked me off, so I couldn't even process what you were saying. But I've been thinking about it and you're right. I'd like you to lead the HR leg of this project. You help me fix this problem, and I'll help you learn how to navigate politically so you don't sabotage what could be a promising career. Sound like a deal?

Karin took her up on her offer, the SVP became an amazing mentor, Karin's career flourished, and attendance improved. When you have a "what were they thinking?" moment, look for the opportunity to Respond with Regard and help the team member grow.

HELP YOUR TEAM UNDERSTAND THE PROCESS: IDEA PATH

Joe has a new microinnovation to improve the business. The idea isn't perfect, but with a tweak or two, it just might solve that problem that's driving everyone nuts. What does Joe do next? If Joe is like half of the people in our research, you'll never hear about it because he assumes no one will do anything with it. But good ideas breed more good ideas. When people see a clear path from idea sharing to implementation, they'll be much more likely to speak up.

On your team, how easy is it for people to bring forward their best ideas? Take a minute to think about this "Idea Path." How does Joe know it's an idea with potential? Have you defined criteria for what a great idea will do for your customers or the team? If not, that's worth thinking through at your next team meeting.

Once Joe determines that his idea is worth sharing, what would he do next? Would he:

- Talk to someone?
- Fill out a card?
- Enter it in a database?
- Schedule a meeting?
- Something else?
- Then what?

We invite you to think about a microinnovation Joe might have—an idea that would incrementally improve efficiency or customer experience in a meaningful way. Consider the Idea Path that this microinnovation would travel. Write down each step Joe would take—including other people's activity necessary to implement the idea. Who would need to authorize it? What levels of approval do different ideas require? How long would each step take?

Every organization's Idea Path is different. We can't spell out the path your microinnovations should travel, but we can help you identify key elements. As you review your Idea Path, look for these common barriers to action. Does your employee:

- Know what successful ideas look like?
- Know what to do with an idea that might work, but isn't perfect?
- Have a realistic understanding of the time frame involved?
- Understand why they need certain approvals?

Teams that consistently improve don't leave the creativity to chance. They have an intentional plan to find good ideas, test, refine, share, and encourage problem solving. Use the Idea Path template in your downloadable *Executive Strategy Guide* to help you, your colleagues, and your team think through how you help ideas move from concept to action.

FIRST TRACKS

Find Five

OBJECTIVES:
- To identify best practices, new ideas, or microinnovations to recognize and celebrate.
- To reinforce and celebrate the Courageous Cultures behaviors and why they are so important.

TIME REQUIRED:
Not much extra; you can do this while you're out and about.

PROCESS:
Your First Tracks to Respond with Regard are to practice seeking out and celebrating contributions. Specifically, work with your team to find and celebrate five contributions. These can be success stories, best practices, and microinnovations. If it happens that someone brings you an idea, even better—Respond with Regard. If you

seek out ideas to celebrate, make sure to recognize at least one contribution that didn't succeed or hasn't been used yet. You want to reinforce the act of thinking and problem solving, not just successful implementation.

CHAPTER 10

Practice the Principle

Never interrupt someone doing something you said couldn't
be done.

— AMELIA EARHART[1]

e thought we were getting ahead of the blizzard. After all,
the snow wasn't predicted to start until Friday. But apparently
we weren't the only ones thinking Thursday morning was a
good time to slip out to our local Trader Joe's. Every register was
open and every line stretched all the way to the back of the store,
but they'd planned for the onslaught of humanity in need of milk,
bread, and Sriracha Seafood Potstickers and had called in
reinforcements.

Knowing that customers weren't happy with the long wait, the
store captain was on the microphone being as merry as possible.
"Hey, everybody, oh my gosh, did you hear it's going to snow?" A
few minutes later, she was back on the mic. "Okay, raise your hand
if you are number seven in your line." We all worked together to
count. It was a nice distraction.

"Wow! Just wow! Today is your special day! Every one of you in
the number seven spot gets a free candy bar." We were number six.
She approached the two people standing behind us, a pair of skinny

seventy-somethings, standing side by side in the number seven spot. She asked them, "Can you share?" They looked at her longingly, and she smiled. "Okay, here's two." She was trying to lighten up a stressful situation. Clearly, she was empowered to influence the customer experience.

After a forty-five-minute wait, we were next in line. The woman in front of us tried to pay with her smartphone, and it crashed the register in our lane (lane eight—which we'd already noted in case there was another contest). They had to call headquarters for IT support. At this point, a free candy bar sounded pretty good. After ten minutes of troubleshooting without success, everyone was getting restless. The jolly captain once again took the microphone: "Okay, we have a lane down so here's what we're going to do. If you're in lane eight, raise your hand."

We were all ears in lane eight and eagerly raised our hands. Everyone else just rolled their eyes. "First thing we're going to do is this. If you are in lane eight, Steve here is going to come by and ask you to name your favorite Trader Joe's item. He's going to go get it for you and you will get that item for free."

Brilliant! At this point, everyone in the store was thinking about which they like more, Popcorn in a Pickle or Uncured Bacon Jam. She continued:

> But here's where the rest of you come in. Some of these folks in lucky lane eight have been waiting for nearly an hour just like you. So, you don't have to do this, but if you would be willing to let them step in front of you, raise both of your hands (yup, that's how deep the snow will be), and you, too, will get your favorite Trader Joe's item for free.

Every line had raised hands, and people began chatting and moving in an orderly fashion—and they all had a good story to tell when they got home. The lady next to us kindly let us step in front of her. We all felt like we'd won the lottery with our free kombucha and ice cream. As the lane seven cashier rang up our order, she was all smiles.

"How great is this?" the cashier asked. "Can you imagine any other grocery store that would respond this way?" We both knew the answer. She grinned with pride and said, "This is why I work here."

It may sound crazy to literally give away the store, but it's working. Trader Joe's doesn't just have customers, they have raving fans, rate at the top of the RPI (Retail Preference Index),[2] and take in more revenue per square foot than any other grocery chain.[3] How do they do it?

If you listen to the *Inside Trader Joe's* podcast, read Mark Gardiner's insider account *Build a Brand Like Trader Joe's*, hang out in the many TJ-centered online forums, or read just about anything written by customers or employees on Trader Joe's culture, you'll quickly find that they train values, like integrity, *kaizen* (continuous self-improvement), and delivering "wow customer service" that makes every shopping experience rewarding, eventful, and fun.[4] They also excel in what we call Practice the Principle.

HOW TO SCALE WHAT WORKS

When you Practice the Principle, you commit to finding the core idea within best practices and help your teams to localize best practices for their unique circumstances. The Trader Joe's store captain is a good example of practicing the principle. The core idea—in this case, a company value—is to provide "wow" customer service. But you can't possibly train or equip people in how to do that in every possible circumstance. Wow customer service is the principle. But they leave exactly how they do that up to the captains, mates, and employees. They're encouraged to Practice the Principle of wow and fun, but to do it in unique ways that would best serve their unique store and community of customers.

Spontaneous contests and giveaways are a localized best practice that made sense in that specific pre-blizzard circumstance. On a slow summer morning with two registers open and only two people in line, customers would probably greet the same contests and giveaways with a curious smile and a shrug. Context matters. As you build your Courageous Culture, the key is to train your team on the values and principles that will guide their innovation and how to refine a best practice for their use.

To Practice the Principle, executives clarify core values and principles, support their leadership teams to review and try out new ideas that align with those principles, and work strategically to improve them. Managers work with their teams to learn from new approaches and identify the principles within their best practices. Employees try new ideas and look for ways to build on them or make them more relevant to their circumstances.

SCALING MICROINNOVATIONS AND BEST PRACTICES

One of the challenges you'll encounter as you get ideas is that a game-changing solution for one team won't work at all in another department. We observed a good example of this challenge in an engineering design firm. Javier was a well-loved director and also an accomplished Italian chef. Every year he would conduct an operational excellence rally that he personally catered with spaghetti made from homemade noodles, handcrafted sausages from wild game he'd hunted, and a sauce he cooked himself with vegetables he'd grown in his garden. It was an annual labor of love for Javier. His team always left the annual rallies energized.

Another director in the same organization confided to us her doubts about her team ever performing like Javier's: "I don't boil water, much less cook like that. Our rallies are flat by comparison. I mean, I'd rather be with Javier's team too." She'd fallen into a common innovation trap that prevents many organizations from scaling their best microinnovations. She'd focused on applying the practice, not the principle.

A principle is a concept that works universally. For instance, treating your customer with respect is a principle of customer service. But the practice of respect can look very different from culture to culture, city to city, and between industries. Cooking a homemade meal for your team is a practice. For most people, that practice isn't transferrable. But the principle of personally investing and connecting to your team is transferrable—every trained leader can do that. You don't scale practices; you scale principles.

PRACTICE THE PRINCIPLE WITH EMPLOYEES

Courageous Culture principles work within your organization as well as in service to your customer. Nestlé's Sonia Studer related how they Practice the Principle of their commitment to diversity and inclusion by ensuring that every market has a specific Diversity and Inclusion action plan localized for that specific market. They reinforce and encourage these localized action plans with "Leading Together" conferences throughout the world, where senior leaders share stories and concrete examples and team members come together to celebrate moments of inclusion throughout the year and make suggestions that lead to concrete actions.

This leadership blend of Cultivate Curiosity, Respond with Regard, and Practice the Principle applied to issues of fundamental human needs creates powerful experiences for employees to speak up and be heard. As Sonia explains, "Involving everyone to contribute to a more diverse and inclusive culture supports an overall Courageous Culture."

HOW TO FIND THE PRINCIPLES IN BEST PRACTICES

When your top performing team seems to have discovered the secret to transform their productivity, customer relationships, or sales, it may be tempting to immediately make everyone in the organization do the same thing. We've worked with many executives who quickly rolled out the new behavior—only to be frustrated with spotty adoption and lackluster results. Leaders can fall into a reactive pattern of running from one great idea to the next, but none of them quite work.

Even if it looks good on paper, your leadership team is on board, and it worked well in the IT war room, field test the change first. Yes, this takes time. This is one of those times it really does work to go slow to go fast. You might be slower out of the gate than others, but when you get it right and everyone owns it, you'll sustain your results and be ready for the next change. The following steps will help you and your leaders identify why a best practice works and how to make it work in other contexts.

1. Ask Why It Works

You can find the principle within a best practice by asking, "Why did this work?" Sometimes you'll have to ask why several times before you get to the essence of what really happened or the fundamental reasons for success. For example, you see John, a customer service rep, consistently getting high scores from his customers. When your manager explores, he discovers that John ignores the opening script your quality team prepared and connects with genuine empathy. Of course, the answer is not to rewrite the script to match what John says. It's to tap into the concept of genuine connection and help all reps get there in their own way.

It takes courage to ask why. You might discover that your breakthrough was really a matter of luck and fortunate timing rather than a repeatable principle everyone can use. That's okay. When you know this from the start, you save everyone the frustration of doing something that doesn't feel right and won't work.

Also, when you help your team members to think critically about their own ideas, they're more likely to find meaningful solutions. Forty percent of our research respondents said they lacked the confidence to share their ideas. Forty-five percent said there's no training in critical thinking and problem solving. When you ask your team to think about why an idea works, you help to address both of these obstacles to building teams of Microinnovators and Customer Advocates.

2. Test the Principle

Once you've found the principle in the best practice, you're ready to test that principle and see if it works the way you and your team think it does. Ideally, when you test the principle, try it in a couple of different settings, with different people. For example, one of our manufacturing clients empowers their teams with 3D printers to experiment with designing and testing new parts to improve their products, which has led to powerful microinnovations they can scale.

3. Listen Closely

This is perhaps the most important part of testing a principle. As you test the principle and roll it out, really listen to what your people tell you. Check in with stakeholders, partners, and customers. Respond to feedback with solutions, not selling. When you fix something, communicate the fix back to the team five times, five different ways. (You'll learn more about 5x5 communication in the next chapter.)

4. Ask How It Can Be Better

As you continue to test and roll out the principle, ask questions that will help refine the principle:

- How can we address challenges that come up and make the change serve its purpose?
- What's working well and how do we leverage it?
- What enhancements do we need?
- Where should we head next?

All these questions help refine the principle—and they also build morale by including employees in your change efforts. At the heart of a Courageous Culture is the idea that great organizations build change together.

LOCALIZE THE PRINCIPLE

One key to successfully refine a best practice is to help your teams work out the principle in ways that make sense and get results in their specific circumstances. This process of localizing principles is central to the Courageous Culture dance between Clarity and Curiosity. Clarity says "this is the principle." Curiosity asks, "How can we work out that principle in the most meaningful way right here, right now?" Recall Karin's sales team. Once they clarified the principle of selling to local small businesses, they got curious about how to do that in a way that made sense across diverse regions. Suits, log cabin lofts, and local outbound sales calls were all localized best practices for the principle of small business sales. But those same behaviors wouldn't work in a different region. Context matters.

Let's take a look at another example of how to localize the principle. Three contact centers were asked to improve their customer experience by increasing the empathy in their representatives' customer interactions. The principle was "more empathy," but each center took a different approach.

Center 1

One center focused on prepaid-phone customers. These customers were often viewed poorly by the service reps. (Their view of who buys prepaid phones was biased based on a small percentage of bad experiences.) The lack of empathy translated to poor customer service. To address the issue, the manager gathered everyone together and showed them a picture of Betty, a kind-looking elderly woman.

He described Betty: "She is a retired nurse. She was a Girl Scout leader for forty years. She was married for fifty-one years to the love of her life—a veteran who died recently. Betty is a prepaid-phone customer. She's also my grandmother. Next time you take a prepaid call, picture Betty on the other end of the line."

"What about Betty?" became a best practice for the principle of empathy. Coaches and team leaders could say "What about Betty?" for an instant boost to customer empathy.

Center 2

The second contact center heard about what the first center had done with their "What about Betty?" campaign. They loved the idea—only one problem: the manager didn't have a grandmother named Betty.

Their leadership team took a look at the principle—a person-focused reminder of what empathy looks like—and came up with their own campaign. Every day for a week, various baby shoes, bibs, bottles, and pacifiers were scattered around the center. Then signs started to appear: "What happened to baby Carl?" People were concerned and intrigued. "Who is baby Carl?" they asked. "And what happened to him?"

At the end of the week, the leadership team pulled everyone together and revealed the meaning behind the baby items. "We know from the conversations this week that you were very concerned about this baby. Well, Carl is an acronym. It stands for Care About Real Lives. When you're struggling for empathy, think about baby CARL."

Then they got an infant-sized baby doll and wrapped it in a blanket. At first, the doll was used to recognize great acts of customer empathy. Soon, however, agents who were tired or struggling with empathy asked to borrow the doll and place it on their desks as a reminder to care about real lives and summon their empathy. This localized approach worked in their center and had a significant impact on their empathy and quality scores. Even so, it would certainly not work in many other environments.

Center 3

The third center went a different way entirely. To increase empathy, they focused on how their leaders would show up with encouragement and empathy to model and support their reps with the same culture they wanted the reps to share with customers. Their best practices included behaviors like all the supervisors lining up as team members arrived for their shifts, then applauding and cheering for them as they entered the center. Team leaders made a point of asking agents "how are you doing?" and listening to the answers, reflecting the emotions they heard—in other words, demonstrating empathy.

All three centers achieved improvements in the customer experience by increasing empathy during calls. But each of them localized the principle in a way that was consistent with their culture and context.

Localizing the principle is an incredibly powerful technique to create ownership, pride, and sticky customer (and employee) experiences. It's not easy for your competitors to mimic because they can't just copy a best practice—it requires careful leadership work to align the principles with your strategic goals and then the local creativity from empowered team members to Practice the Principle in ways that are relevant and make sense.

To reinforce localization, actively look for and tell stories about how people use the same idea in different ways. How are different teams living out the idea in their daily work? When you find and celebrate these different activities and reinforce the underlying principle, it helps everyone think creatively about how they might do it.

REFINING AN IDEA THAT JUST MIGHT WORK

If you've eaten an apple in the United States recently, there's a good chance it was a Honeycrisp (David's personal favorite). Honeycrisps are known for their crunch and combination of tart sweetness. They also retail for double or triple the normal price of an apple. Apple growers produced the original Honeycrisp apple tree in the 1960s and '70s—but then threw it out in 1977 because it looked like the trees would have problems making it through the winter. Two years later, a man named David Bedford found a few clones of that original tree that had somehow survived. He was impressed with the fruit and thought it had a chance to succeed.

Winter hardiness wasn't the Honeycrisps only challenge. Birds love them as much as humans do, so growing them required extra bird netting. They need higher levels of calcium in the soil. And the fruit can't go straight from the tree to refrigeration—it requires a week of adjustment once it's picked.[5] In a low-margin, competitive retail market these might seem like insurmountable problems. Growing the Honeycrisp would cost more. The only way it would work is if customers would pay more—a seemingly impossible barrier in the competitive apple market. And yet, customers today willingly pay two to three times more for a Honeycrisp apple than an averaged-priced apple. All because Bedford and his team asked "what if"—What if this could work?

The Honeycrisp was a microinnovation—it's still an apple, after all. But sometimes a small improvement can revolutionize a market. Does your team have any Honeycrisp ideas hanging around, waiting for someone to take a chance and ask, "What if this could work?" When you look at an idea that has merit and "just might work" but that also comes with a number of challenges, go back to Cultivate Curiosity. The "how can we" question is particularly helpful here: "How can we make this apple viable? Well, we could charge more. But would people pay it? I'm not sure, but we can test that and find out." Imagine if Karin's team, after one successful Small Business Madness Tuesday, had shrugged and said, "Yeah, this was good, but there are too many barriers. We're not business salespeople." No transformation, no awards, no massive customer growth. To refine an idea that just might work, ask, "How can we?" and test your answers. You never know what you'll find.

FIRST TRACKS

Identify the Principle

OBJECTIVES:
- To determine best practices with the opportunity to scale—and to determine how to make them transferrable.
- To practice identifying the principle within a best practice.

TIME REQUIRED:
About an hour.

PROCESS:
Review some of the best practices you discovered in your work in Chapter 9. As your team reviews what's working, help them to

identify and extract the principle from the best practice. Here are a few questions you can use.

- In what circumstances is this an ideal best practice?
- Are these circumstances different from team to team?
- Why does this practice achieve such good results?
- In our organization, what is defined and must be consistent from team to team? (For example, brand standards, regulations and legal requirements, and strategic objectives that you identified in the Know step of the Clarity phase.)
- What's different from context to context (team to team, place to place, other)?
- What is the core behavior or activity that will work across teams and regions and how might it look different in those different contexts?

CHAPTER 11

Galvanize the Genius

"Go back?" he thought. "No good at all! Go sideways? Impossible! Go forward? Only thing to do! On we go!" So up he got, and trotted along with his little sword held in front of him and one hand feeling the wall, and his heart all of a patter and a pitter.

—J. R. R. TOLKIEN, *The Hobbit*[1]

Rick, a service manager in a large home-services organization, had mastered the foundational Clarity phase of the Courageous Cultures Cycle. He'd met with his team to emphasize their strategic priority—delight customers on every installation. He'd explained why it was so important—they were a premium service provider in a commoditized industry—and service was their only differentiator. Rick was clear that he wanted their ideas and best practices on how to take service to the next level.

He'd spent time with his technicians Cultivating Curiosity about how they could deliver premium service. As they came up with ideas, he Responded with Regard and then Practiced the Principle by brainstorming and prioritizing the specific behaviors they could commit to on every visit (for example, take off their shoes before entering the home; call the customer by name; leave the workspace better than they found it). The technicians created and owned the performance criteria. The plan was easily understood, easy to implement, and the team owned it.

Two weeks later, Rick was out on a series of ride-alongs with his techs. And guess what? Not a single person consistently did what they had all agreed to do just a few weeks before. He called us in frustration: "We spent so much time coming up with those commitments and everyone was engaged. What happened?"

Rick's dilemma is common. As anyone who's ever made a New Year's resolution knows, human behavior easily reverts back to normal unless we do something to reinforce the change. In the Courageous Cultures Cycle, it isn't enough to do the work in the Curiosity phase without looping back to Clarity to Galvanize the Genius. We love the word galvanize in this context because it has two separate meanings,[2] both of which you'll want in your culture.

First, galvanize means to "excite someone into action"—and that's certainly what you and your team want to happen with all the genius ideas you've discovered. Galvanize has a second relevant meaning as well: it's the process where iron or steel is treated with a protective layer of zinc in order to prevent rust and corrosion. In Courageous Cultures, corrosion looks like that slide back to old behaviors or safe silence. None of that. It's time to Galvanize the Genius: to excite your team to action and prevent the slow decline of the culture you've all worked so hard to build.

HOW TO GALVANIZE THE GENIUS

When leaders struggle to maintain new cultural norms, there are usually three areas that cause trouble. Problems in one or more of these areas make it difficult for people to commit to new behaviors and undermine their willingness to share new ideas—why waste time thinking or speaking up when nothing will change? But when you and your leaders master these three elements, you can rapidly respond to changing circumstances, quickly adapt new principles, and react to customer needs before your competition has started to look for a solution. The three elements to galvanize your genius are Know, Flow, and Show.

Know means to clearly articulate what success looks like and the fundamental behaviors that make it happen. *Flow* is your ability to translate vision into behaviors and ensure all employees understand what they're doing, why they're doing it, and how their work fits into the big picture. *Show* is about demonstrating that leaders and team members know what to do, do it well, and address unforeseen challenges before the rust sets in. Let's take a closer look at each of these elements and how to implement them to reinforce your Courageous Culture.

Know

"We're doing a great job responding to customer needs, but when it comes to compliance, we're dropping the ball." Monica, a senior vice president, came to us for help getting her team aligned with industry regulations. "It won't matter how wonderful our customer experience is if we don't take care of these basics. We've got to be 100 percent compliant and we've got to get there fast." As we worked with Monica's team, we discovered a great culture filled with Customer Advocates who were on fire, looking for better ways to serve the customer. They'd built formalized systems to Cultivate Curiosity and solicit employees' ideas, and they consistently celebrated team members for finding creative solutions to customer problems.

But in their zeal to creatively serve customers and respond to the variety of issues they faced every day, the leadership team had lost sight of some fundamentals. They lacked Clarity about context, about what mattered most, and the order in which to achieve their goals. As a result, employees were working hard—just not at what mattered most in that moment. Even in Courageous Cultures, you've got to follow the rules.

Has this ever happened to you? You get everyone focused on doing what's right for the customer—and a few well-meaning folks, trying to do the right thing, lose sight of the bigger picture? In your first loop through the Clarity phase of the Courageous

Culture Cycle, you focused on identifying a clear strategic goal, clarified your values, connected what you're asking to why you were asking it, and checked for understanding to make sure everyone's on the same page. In your First Tracks, you created a vision for your Courageous Culture and identified the behaviors you would see. As you cycle back to Clarity, you'll renew that vision and incorporate the ideas, solutions, and best practices you and your team have discovered.

Monica's team excelled at Curiosity, but when it came to the Courageous Cultures dance, they'd ignored Clarity about compliance for too long. Additionally, many team members could conceptually explain the importance of compliance, but very few could describe how they contributed to it in their daily work. As we worked with their senior leadership team to clarify what mattered most and how everyone would incorporate these priorities in their daily work, one executive said it well: "No wonder everyone's confused. We don't really know what this means for us—how do we expect our teams to do it?"

When we talk about the continual need to renew Clarity and ensure everyone's on the same page, leaders often get frustrated. You may even be thinking, "Do I really have to explain this? Shouldn't they just get it?" We hear you. You're moving fast. You're thinking big and your priorities make sense to you. You need people who can keep up, get on the same wavelength, and move quickly. The challenge is that even talented, motivated people understand the same ideas differently. And unless your leadership team and managers know how the strategic goals translate into daily behaviors, you'll stay stuck.

Clear direction creates the foundation for trust, decision-making, and innovation. Monica and her team needed every manager and employee to understand how vital compliance was to customer care. Everyone needed a clear understanding of how to live out compliance in their daily work. And they needed to establish this Clarity without losing the beautiful aspects of their customer-centered culture they had worked so hard to build. They didn't want to go backward while moving forward. They leveraged their culture of Curiosity to get serious about Clarity.

There's no better way to showcase what's most important than to isolate the conversation, which they did through what we call "know meetings." The executive team met and established clear outcomes for their compliance strategy. Then each VP held a day-long Clarity-focused strategic planning session with their direct report team to define what compliance meant for their teams, to identify the top priorities that would ensure 100 percent compliance (education, training, cross-departmental collaboration), and build tight action plans to get there—fast.

The magic of these "know meetings" is that the knowing wasn't a one-way lecture. In Courageous Cultures, knowing doesn't mean *you* know everything—your job is to make sure that the most important things are known. Monica's team needed to talk through what each team specifically needed to do, what obstacles and conflicts were most likely to interfere, and how to resolve them. Before anything else, they needed to be 100 percent compliant with all of their industry's rules and regulations.

Monica wanted her teams to know that compliance was vital while maintaining an extraordinary customer experience. As you get curious and identify new principles and best practices, can your leaders clearly articulate what success looks like and the behaviors that will make it happen?

Flow

Let's get back to Rick, whose team of technicians had worked together to decide the behaviors that would deliver premium service. Rick's challenge was that he'd taken a "one and done" approach to communication. Until you've mastered the Clarity-Curiosity dance with consistent messaging, your team is likely to fall back into old routines. It's frustrating, but it's normal human behavior—and one of the most common causes of executive frustration. How do you compete with all the noise and ensure everyone knows what matters most, knows why it's important, and stays focused on the vital areas to get curious about improving?

Flow means that everyone is aligned with strategic goals, understands what matters most, and knows what to do to succeed. To achieve that level of Clarity, executives communicate strategic priorities and behaviors that bring success. Managers model these success behaviors, translate organizational goals into department and team goals, and equip their teams to succeed. Employees demonstrate success behaviors and ensure they understand the why behind the work. When you successfully flow Clarity to every corner of your organization, innovation, problem solving, and customer advocacy—not to mention accountability and breakthrough results—become much easier. But as Rick realized, communication isn't a single event. Rick's team was clear about what mattered most, but as they returned to their daily work, habit and routine took over.

5X5 COMMUNICATION

The antidote to inertia and the gravitational pull of routine is 5x5 communication. This means you communicate mission critical information five times, five different ways. People build memories, meaning, and significance with what they see or hear regularly— that's why we encourage you to communicate five times. Have you ever driven down a street you've been down a hundred times, looked up and seen an intriguing new restaurant? You go in and find out that it's been there for six years, but you'd just never noticed it before. That's why we invite you to communicate five different ways. People tune in—and tune out—different types of communication.

To implement 5x5 communication, Rick took the key behaviors that they'd agreed to and built a five-week reinforcement plan. Each behavior got a week-long spotlight where he reinforced it five times, five different ways throughout the week.

For example, "Take off your shoes" week involved:

- Pictures of muddy boots with a big X over them posted on the steering wheel of each truck.
- A Monday morning huddle reminder.
- Quick text message reminders to the team distribution list.
- Ride-alongs with each tech to reinforce removing their shoes.
- Follow-up calls with customers that resulted in recognition (or accountability).

Rick told us how, at the end of week five, when he went to reinforce the behaviors again, the techs shouted, "We know, we know." Rick smiled. "That's how I knew I had finally gotten through."

As you're working on your 5x5 communication plan, think beyond emails and conference calls. Keep in mind that, outside of work, your team consumes information in social soundbites and pithy podcasts, and an answer to almost every question is a YouTube search away. Your team is accustomed to people showing up human, without scripts, sharing their insights as if they're talking to a trusted friend. There are many creative ways to vary your 5x5 communication. Here are a couple of techniques to interrupt your communication-as-usual:

- **Strategic storytelling.** Start with the message you're looking to reinforce and then wrap a personal story around it to share with your team.
- **Internal podcasts.** Imagine being able to sit next to your front-line managers as they drive to work and share your strategic vision and insights and talk about what's keeping you up at night. That's exactly what an internal podcast can do for you.
- **Informal video.** It doesn't have to be perfect to be effective. Imagine if you recorded a two-minute Monday morning video

and shared it with your team, or a Friday recap of highlights of the week. Keep it pithy and fun with one clear message you want to reinforce.

- **Operations excellence rallies.** These highly interactive meetings take townhalls to the next level, where you start with a strategic priority, use a strategic story to reinforce why it's important, share a compelling business case, do a bit of recognition, then get the team learning and sharing, practicing very practical skills they can go back and apply immediately. Karin leveraged this technique as part of her 5x5 communication strategy in the sales team transformation we shared in Chapter 6.

- **Handwritten notes.** We've met several CEOs who use weekly handwritten notes to thank team members for their work. This is an opportunity to reinforce a new practice, stretch goal, or company value. One of our clients shared, "I have always been a big believer in handwritten notes. Now that I'm being more intentional about building our culture, in my written notes I'm deliberately linking what they did back to one of our five strategic company values. I think that's making them even more meaningful."

When it comes to communication, once is never enough. To change behavior, you've got to ensure that you and your managers are communicating five times, five different ways. Don't let anyone miss the message.

FIVE REASONS YOUR HIGH PERFORMERS
RESIST YOUR NEW IDEA

Do you have a talented team of top performers who don't seem to be running with the latest innovation or great idea you've introduced to the team? When you're struggling to Galvanize the Genius, check to see if any of these issues are at play.

They question your motives.

The best way to ensure your team trusts your motives is to question them yourself first. Is your great idea really an edict you're passing along from above that you know won't work but you're too afraid to speak up? Do you spend more time on how the project looks than on how the project works? Be sure your motives are sound.

They're still actively working to make your last great idea work.

Strong performers don't want to disappoint you, so they might be scared to "complain." But being overwhelmed is often real.

Your great idea is a great idea, but it won't work here.

If one of your managers has cracked the code, you think, "Why not require everyone to do it the same way and exponentially improve your results?" Be sure that the best practice you want to adopt makes sense in different circumstances.

Your great idea isn't so great.

One of the biggest mistakes we see well-intentioned, energetic leaders make is requiring large-scale execution on an idea before thinking through the details. Great ideas do no good if they don't work in real life. Before moving to implementation, pause to ask questions like:

• How's everyone feeling about this idea?
• How do you think our customers will respond to this change?
• What do you think are the biggest challenges we will face making this happen?

- What do we need to consider to ensure this will be a huge success?

Your great idea is only your idea.

When you build a Courageous Culture filled with Problem Solvers and Microinnovators, they'll want to be engaged. If you're the one having all the great ideas, the culture isn't going to feel very courageous. It might be time to step back, pose the opportunities or challenges, and ask for their ideas. You can always refine their suggestions, Practice the Principle—and now you've got shared ownership.

Show

Steve had thrown every ounce of energy into launching their new initiative. Everyone knew what was important and why, and his 5x5 communication strategy was more like 30x30. Everyone in every corner of the company knew the goals and mission-critical behaviors. He had the most talented people working on the strategy and had committed massive financial resources to see it through. But the program struggled to gain traction. As Steve tells it:

I was getting so frustrated about the lack of sales from our new strategic program, I had reinforced why this was so important to our company so many times, I was sick of hearing myself talk about it. But the service reps were struggling to convert inquiries to sales.

Then one day, I went into the contact center and took a few customers' calls myself. The questions were tough. I realized our new program was difficult to explain and our training had not prepared our reps to take those calls. No amount of explaining to our reps why this program mattered would help until they knew how to answer our customers' questions.

We've worked with many organizations where leaders do the hard work getting to know what's important and flow it well throughout the organization, but then they don't finish by showing that it's actually happening. How you finish what you start makes all the difference between good intentions and great implementations. Finish strong and you kick off a virtuous cycle of good morale, results, and more trust in your leaders. Failing to finish does just the opposite: morale tanks, results languish, and leaders' credibility erodes. Sadly, organizations are littered with leaders who start but never finish.

Steve wasn't able to Galvanize the Genius until he got out with people and really understood how the initiatives worked, where they were stuck, and how to move them forward. *Show* means that you measure and inspect outcomes and behaviors at every level of the business. You and your team are certain where the desired behaviors are happening and where they break down—both through quantitative analysis and direct observation. You ensure that managers are reinforcing behaviors through celebration and accountability, and employees are doing what they've committed to do.

Keep in mind that demonstrating results isn't just a matter of ensuring that everything is going according to plan. We worked with a financial services organization that had a very people-focused culture where a senior vice president reflected on a meeting we'd facilitated: "I think it was surprising for everyone, the extent to which people in the room wanted more feedback about their leadership and performance, and how much they were struggling to get it." People, at every level, benefit from clear feedback and the confidence that they're heading in the right direction.

When it comes to demonstrating results, there are two common problems leaders experience: blind trust and lost trust. Leaders who trust blindly assume that because everyone has understood and agreed, everything will happen as it should. They neglect to follow up because they get busy, they worry that inspecting conveys mistrust, or they don't think they should have to follow up. Leaders who lose trust as they follow up typically focus exclusively on the numbers and neglect to lead the human beings on their team. A healthy Show will help your leaders avoid either of these problems and Galvanize the Genius you've worked so hard to build.

TRUST, BUT VERIFY

Leaders who trust blindly forget that accountability doesn't happen by chance. Life is busy for everyone on your team. People have more to do than time to do it. Their plan will get interrupted and then the interruptions will be interrupted. Without an intentional, focused way to finish what you start, your team's plan won't happen. Help your leaders choose to finish, but don't leave it to chance or a heroic act of willpower.

If your leaders have to spend energy trying to remember everything they need to finish, they'll never do it. There's just too much going on, and thinking about every open loop can be exhausting. To hold everyone accountable for what matters most, schedule the Show. When the team sets an intention or defines a key behavior, make an appointment with yourself to inspect the outcomes, review the desired behaviors, and ensure that the 5x5 communication happened. For senior leaders, the most important Show is to ensure that leaders and managers at every level fully engage in the Clarity phase. Are your leaders practicing 5x5 communication and modeling success?

For ongoing accountability, the key is when—when will it happen? What moment in time will you and your leaders follow up, follow through, and finish? You can schedule a site visit, a skip-level meeting, or, like Steve, you can dive in and participate alongside your team. The leaders who do this best master the art of the old Russian proverb made famous by Ronald Reagan and now repeated in conference rooms around the world: "Trust, but verify."

GET IN THE ARENA

Leaders who micromanage, care only about metrics, and forget to lead people quickly lose people's trust. One way to overcome this challenge is when you head out to Show that everything is going according to plan, be prepared to learn otherwise. The willingness to see what was really happening—and why—made Steve's Show meaningful. He knew the importance of seeing and experiencing the work firsthand. This is what bestselling author and vulnerability and courage expert Brené Brown calls "being in the arena."[3]

> "If you're not in the arena, also getting your ass kicked, I'm not interested in your feedback."
> —Brené Brown

To truly understand the support his team needed, Steve had to experience the initiative from the front line and hear from customers. His frontline employees were much more interested in hearing his sales ideas when they knew that he knew how hard it was—and that he was vulnerable enough to admit it. In companies where the Show phase breaks down, we often hear complaints that "leaders aren't in the arena."

For example:

- "If a meeting is going to be contentious, my boss always finds a way to send me instead of going herself. And when I get back, she's full of feedback of how I could have positioned our argument differently."
- "My manager is too scared to advocate for what we need; she puts politics over progress every time. We work around her and tell her as little as possible."
- "We're trying to get this project moving, but we're all getting different marching orders from our supervisors. When we suggest they work out the issues at their level, they say the decisions are bigger than them and they don't want to make waves."

If you're inspecting without being "in the arena" or not putting yourself out there for your team or not on the front line to know what really happens, you won't be able to celebrate true success or have the credibility to influence change. Ensuring that your leaders follow through on their commitments is as important as celebrating success. When you find a team that can't explain why they're doing what they're doing (or they aren't doing the right things at all), start with their leader. Clarify what success looks like, reestablish the 5x5 communication plan, and schedule your next Show.

When we share the Know, Flow, Show method to help leaders Galvanize the Genius, we often hear some form of "That's a lot of work. If we hire good people, can't we just depend on them to do their job?" Yes, you can depend on them—but in a Courageous Culture, everyone's work is more than the routine assignments that a computer could do faster, more accurately, and for less money. When you bring the human elements of creativity, problem solving, empathy, and collaboration together to better serve your customers, you also get the human differences in personality, distraction, competing priorities, and barriers to communication. That's where the rust can creep in and why we need to Galvanize the Genius with clear communication and a consistent, strong finish.

FIRST TRACKS

Your Communication Plan

Now it's time to take the principle you explored and Galvanize the Genius with a communication plan that ensures Clarity and results.

OBJECTIVE:
- To ensure that your chosen microinnovation, solution, or best practice is transmitted accurately and implemented throughout your team.

TIME REQUIRED:
- Fifteen to thirty minutes to build communication plan.
- Ten to thirty days to implement plan.

PROCESS:

Working with your team, complete the following communication plan.

KNOW **What matters** **most** (for example, deliver premium service with these three behaviors . . .)					
FLOW **Your 5x5** **communication** **strategy** (team meetings, emails, posters, informal videos, company off-site meetings)					
SHOW **That it's** **happening** (e.g., MBWA, site visits, peer recognition program)					

Step 1: Know—When completing the Know section, clarify what success looks like for the implementation of the microinnovation, solution, or principle you want to communicate.

Step 2: Flow—In the Flow section, identify five different methods you and your team will use to communicate what you clarified in the Know section. These five different methods should happen at five different times—usually over the space of ten to thirty days. Be sure to identify specifically who will do what and when.

Step 3: Show—Complete the Show section with the strategies you will use to ensure implementation takes place and to surface any challenges. Be sure to identify specifically who will do what and when.

Once you complete the plan, implement it.

CHAPTER 12

How to Build an Infrastructure for Courage

If I'm ever in doubt about whether a leader is making a positive impact on my organization, I ask myself this most important question, Would I want my child working for this person? If the answer is no, I know I need to make the tough call.

—DAVID ALEXANDER, President, Soliant

Karin walked toward the makeshift outsourced contact center housed in what had, until recently, been a retail store in a strip mall. The center had been opened so quickly that you could still make out the name of the store it replaced by the dust left behind from the letters that had been removed. Karin cringed as she realized the dressing room was being used as a coaching room. The sea of cubes all looked the same, there were no personal pictures, and the walls were stark, with the exception of stack-ranked quality scores thumbtacked to the conference room wall. Hoping to make a human connection and learn from the most successful agents, Karin looked at the names topping the quality list. She asked Rich, the center director, "Can I speak to Sarah, John, and Tavon?"

"Oh no, those three agents all resigned last week. Let me see who is still here," Rich said nervously. "Yeah, uh, this is an old report." He flipped through the pages. "It's not always accurate. But this center is going to be great! I have an amazing team and all the support I need. Don't worry, I'm sure we'll be making our objectives by next month."

Karin then met with the supervisors. To a person they all said, "We love it here!" "It's a great place to work," and "You can count on us!" Which of course was the worst sign of all. Everyone had clearly been coached to stay positive and not discuss the real challenges they faced. The FOSU was palpable.

Karin moved on to visit the next center. As she pulled her rental car into the parking lot, the center director, Fred, said, "Let me meet you in the parking lot. I want you to start like I do each day. I always begin my morning in the parking lot and think about what it's like for our agents the moment they walk in the door."

The entrance walls were brightly painted and agents were greeted by supervisors as they started their shift. Further into the center, each team had cubes with a different theme: some with baby pictures of the agents with a "guess who" game; others with commitment statements from each agent declaring what they would do to wow their customers; and others with pretty graphs of bad results that were trending slightly in the right direction.

"You've got to see the coaching room!" Fred led Karin to a room with lava lamps, bean bag chairs, candy dishes, speakers to listen to calls, and a whiteboard for brainstorming. As they sat down to plan the rest of the visit, Fred said:

I've got to be honest with you. We hardly get to use this room. There's no time. We agreed to ramp up this center far too quickly and we bit off more than we could chew. It was way harder to recruit the right talent, particularly at the supervisor level, than we thought.

Some of the supervisors are agents we hired just last month whom we had to promote because the center is growing so fast. They haven't been properly trained. Because everyone's so new, the calls are too long, and we can't take as many as we agreed to, so everyone's working overtime. People are tired. There's no time for training or coaching.

Even if it means making less money, I need time to take my agents off the phones to better support them. We're not getting all the data we need to make decisions, so I'm operating a bit in the dark. I've asked my supervisors to meet with you and tell you the truth about where we're struggling, what we're working on, and where we need your help. We need to talk about how the way these contracts are structured and what that means in terms of how we can invest in our agents and give you the quality you need.

Two outsourced contact centers. Both had agreed to ramp up too quickly in order to win work that they weren't prepared to handle. Both were in deep trouble, providing a terrible customer experience and suffering from high attrition. One chose to eke out any margin they could by ignoring infrastructure and attempting to disguise the glaring problems that no one wanted to talk about. The other knew that the only chance of survival was to invest in infrastructure, get past their FOSU, and partner on a sustainable plan.

Guess which center made a fast turnaround and which center closed three months later?

Karin and the leadership team continued to have similar courageous conversations with the executives of the other outsourced contact centers to clearly define success and talk frankly about the infrastructure needed for sustained success. They slowed down their growth to a sustainable pace, revisited the contracts to give more time for coaching and training, introduced a new coaching approach, improved reporting, and substantially upped the recognition and support. They even closed each center for a few hours to have high-energy, fun kickoff rallies each year to ensure every employee understood what was most important and why, to celebrate progress, to share best practices, and to recognize top performers.

Perhaps the most courageous act of all was that the executives from each of the competing companies agreed to come together to meet and share nonproprietary best practices for employee engagement and support. The result? Almost every center achieved parity in quality with internal centers. This was a dramatic improvement that many people thought could never happen. Attrition lessened substantially and that built a foundation to open more centers. A win-win for all involved.

You can't fix infrastructure issues if everyone's too scared to speak the truth. And you can't possibly build a Courageous Culture without the infrastructure to support it. What people see and experience affects what they do far more than what they hear a leader say. Every system either fuels or frustrates your strategy and culture.

To build an infrastructure for courage, pay special attention to how:

- You recruit and hire.
- Prospective team members experience your company before they arrive.
- New additions experience the company as they arrive.
- You compensate, recognize, and treat people while they are a part of the company.
- Employees receive performance feedback.
- You equip people with the skills they need to succeed.
- You choose leaders—and how you equip them.

The dance between Clarity and Curiosity can infuse every aspect of your systems. Let's take a look at how you can ensure these core systems help you build an infrastructure that cultivates courage in your culture.

RECRUITING AND HIRING

Violet recruited Brian into the general manager role because of his long track record of success at an established Fortune 500 firm. Her company was on a trajectory of fast growth, so she wanted Brian to help them raise their game. In the interview, he shared lots of best practices from his old company. Brian's previous employer was known for its best-in-class training and consistent customer service. The more Violet heard in the interview, the more excited she was. Brian was perfect for the job. Until he wasn't.

As it turns out, Brian thrived in a high-Clarity culture. When handed a playbook, he knew exactly what to do. And did it flawlessly. But in the whirlwind of a fast-growing start-up, he was completely lost. He had trouble transferring what he had learned in his old role to his new job. Frustrated by the lack of guidelines and procedures, he kept going to his boss for help in making every little decision. He was too overwhelmed to innovate. He was lucky to just get through the day. In the interview, Violet had been so focused on what his company was doing, she didn't get a good sense of Brian's capacity to replicate it on his own.

On the rebound from Brian, Violet went in a different direction. This time she hired Sal, a bright millennial with tons of ideas. Sal was the poster child of can-do energy. He had been wildly successful in his last gig at a company known for their innovative culture—because he had a right-hand guy who operationalized his ideas. Without that guy, Sal was lost. Violet had been so impressed with Sal's energy and charisma in the interview that she forgot to ask him about his role in actually making those ideas come to life.

Has that ever happened to you? You deliberately recruit from a company with the culture you're looking to create. Your prospective recruit looks great on paper. She has a tremendous track record of success. But within the first ninety days, you know you've made a wrong choice.

When it comes to hiring managers with courage and the ability to innovate and execute with Clarity, it seems to make sense to fish where the fish are—to identify companies with cultures that do this well and to search for the leaders who make it happen. But make sure you also dig a level deeper to ensure your candidates have done the same work you need them to do, in similar circumstances to what they'll encounter in your organization.

Ideally, your candidate will be competent on both sides of the Clarity-Curiosity dance that are vital to build a Courageous Culture. Or you can put together integrated teams with complementary skill sets. For entry-level or frontline positions, revisit your traditional postings and job descriptions that emphasize compliant work but are silent about solving problems or looking out for the customer. Who are your recruiters looking for? If you have a team with an exemplary Courageous Culture, identify the core traits and competencies that make the team work. Incorporate those traits and competencies into your job descriptions and recruiting.

COURAGEOUS CULTURE INTERVIEW QUESTIONS

During interviews, do your people ask behavior-based questions about prospective employees' experiences solving problems, seeing through the customer's eyes, and making small improvements in their day-to-day work? Here are a few structured interview questions that will help you dig a level deeper with your candidate to gauge their experience in contributing to and building a Courageous Culture.

Their Track Record of Courage and Innovation

- What's the best idea you've ever had to improve the business? Tell me about the idea. What did you do with it and what happened as a result?
- Tell me about a time that you strongly disagreed with your manager. What was the issue? How did you work to resolve the conflict?
- Describe the most difficult problem you've ever faced at work. How did you work to overcome it? What are you most proud of about your approach and what would you do differently the next time?

- What's the biggest mistake you've ever made at work? What did you learn?

Leading Others to Be Courageous and Innovative

- Have you ever led a team through a large-scale change? What was it? Describe the process you took. What was the result?
- What techniques do you use to encourage employees to share ideas to improve the business?
- In this company, we require every employee to think and act like a Customer Advocate. Have you led teams like that? How did you know that team members were solving problems and acting on behalf of your customers?
- How do you build problem-solving and critical-thinking skills in your employees? Tell me about your biggest success story in this arena.

COURAGE IN ONBOARDING

Karin recently had lunch with Will, one of her all-time favorite direct reports. They'd met to talk about his new job. Will was visibly frustrated as he described the situation: "Well, basically my week of new hire orientation ended with my boss saying, 'I didn't hire you for your ideas. I hired you to implement mine.'"

Seeing the look of surprise on Karin's face, Will continued, "But I've been thinking about it. I probably came on a bit too strong. I had so many ideas right out of the gate, I think I overwhelmed him and maybe even hurt his feelings. He thought I was being critical rather than trying to help. From now on, I'm keeping my mouth shut and working on my exit strategy."

Which is tragic. Because Will's not just an idea guy, he's a loyal operations manager who will do anything to make your vision happen—including finding creative ways to accelerate results. Surely, he'd been hired for his track record of success, and yet somehow, they had lost him at hello.

Sixty-seven percent of our research participants said management operates according to the notion that "this is the way we've always done it." You can dispel that myth on their first day. Start by making it perfectly clear that speaking up is what "people like us" do. Be clear that sharing best practices and speaking up is an integral part of your culture. For example:

> Around here, speaking up when you see a problem or have an idea is a vital part of the job. We expect you to be on the constant lookout for how to make things better for our customers, easier, or more effective. The most successful employees are Microinnovators and Problem Solvers.

That's just a start. It's likely that your new hires have not experienced a true Courageous Culture and they'll be skeptical. Be sure to showcase specific examples of employees at all levels who came up with great ideas that changed the game. You can have employees come and share their stories or create a video where employees tell their stories of their idea and the impact it had, or how they found and solved a problem.

This gives you a two-for-one infrastructure bump because it also serves as recognition and encouragement for people who speak up. While you're sharing these success stories, also include some great ideas that didn't work. You want your new hires to understand that failing doesn't mean having an idea that didn't work—it's *not* thinking and *not* contributing that leads to failure.

We also recommend that you include training in critical thinking and problem solving at an appropriate level for their role. Remember that 45 percent of the employees in our research said they hadn't been trained. Introducing them to some of the simple tools like the IDEA framework or the nine "Whats" coaching model from Chapter 14 can be a good start.

Once you've worked through Clarity about your expectations for speaking up and given your new hires starter tools, get curious. Tap into the best practices and ideas they bring from their last organization. Carve out dedicated time to ask what they liked most about working at their last job and why. If your new hires have worked in your industry before, even better—dig deep to learn how other companies approach your biggest challenges.

As you start looking for their best ideas, be aware that your new hires may not have enough context to know which best practices are needed right out of the gate. They might assume you already do what they considered to be business as usual at their last job. Then they're surprised to learn that you're not doing that at all. You can overcome this gap and benefit from your new hires' previous experiences when you give them a straightforward assignment.

During their first month on the job, ask them to write down at least three new ideas or best practices they would recommend. You can help structure this homework with a few conversation starters:

- How did they approach (insert your biggest challenge here) at your previous company?
- What does XYZ company do better than we do?
- What tools or processes do you miss from your old company?
- If you could teach everyone here one best practice from your previous job, what would that be?

Then make an appointment to follow up with them to discuss their ideas one month later. This final step is so important because you are both reinforcing the expectation for innovation and immediately tapping into their outsider's perspective. Keep in mind how to Respond with Regard: if they may make a suggestion that won't work, thank them for thinking about it, and give them the additional information they need. Now, starting from their first month at work, you have another strategic thinker.

BUILDING A TRAINING PLAN

The skills we've been talking about throughout this book are not intuitive for most people. (If they were, everyone would do them—it's easier to do what we've always known than to respond to a changing world.) New skills require training, consistent reinforcement, and application to real business challenges—starting with your executive team.

Does your senior leadership team have the executive training and tools to establish a clear vision and translate behaviors throughout their organizations? Do they have a clear plan to mine for microinnovations and consistently recognize and reinforce best practices? Be sure your executive level development includes time for them to build their Courageous Cultures implementation strategy—including how they will measure progress.

One of Amy Edmondson's most important findings about psychological safety at work is that it happens at the team level. Two teams working at the same company with all the same infrastructure can have radically different levels of FOSU and, consequently, different levels of microinnovations, problem solving, and customer advocacy depending on their manager.

A common mistake leaders make when trying to build a Courageous Culture is that they ask their managers to run before they've learned to walk. Before you work on training anything too fancy, be sure your managers have the fundamental skills to build trust and influence. Do they:

- Have the competence and tools to set and reinforce clear expectations?
- Hold accountability conversations in a way that builds results and relationships?
- Regularly celebrate success and encourage their people?
- Connect with their employees at a human level?
- Run effective meetings that translate into meaningful results?

- Hold meaningful and regular one-on-one meetings with their team members?

Once these foundations are in place, you can help them to master the Curiosity phase of the Courageous Cultures Cycle with ways to think more strategically and critically, the skill to ask courageous questions, replicate best practices, and encourage more ideas from their teams.

And if you're serious about building a Courageous Culture and want to make it easier for your managers to Cultivate Curiosity and find good ideas, don't overlook the importance of training your frontline employees on some consistent behaviors and techniques. Overcommunicate the big picture so they have Clarity about your strategic goals and what successful ideas would accomplish. Define what being a Customer Advocate means for their roles and let them explore what that looks like in different scenarios. Train them on how to vet their ideas and communicate them well.

RECOGNITION AND REWARDS

"Can't they just work it out?" John yelled.

John was a gruff, hardworking engineer who had built a global hardware and software manufacturing company from the ground up. As CEO, his firm had enjoyed a market-leading position for decades. Now its reputation was slipping, customer complaints piled up, and the new product they needed to ship to maintain their market share looked like it would be many months late. Gene, the vice president of engineering, and Kathy, the vice president of sales, and their teams, had been battling one another for months, and John had called David for help rallying his team to make up ground.

"They won't be able to work it out," David replied. "Not until everyone is clear about what matters most."

"But I can't be any clearer! We've got to make up ground and get the new product in customers' hands. What's so hard to understand?"

"So, engineering should focus exclusively on the new product?"

"That's right."

"At what cost?"

John frowned. "What do you mean, at what cost?"

"Well, every day that engineering won't address customer complaints, your sales team is losing customers. The sales team is evaluated and paid based on customer retention and commissions for an unsupported product. They hear what you say is most important, but the system they're working in says something else, and they're worried they won't have customers left to sell the new product."

John sat down and looked at the ceiling. "So, they can't work it out because . . ."

"Because you're sending two very different messages about what matters most."

At the highest level, the words were clear: "Get the new product to market quickly." But one of the reasons the company struggled to get there was that their compensation, recognition, and reward systems weren't aligned with the strategic goal. The sales team's compensation and bonus structure required time from engineering to solve customer issues with the older products. Time they couldn't get until they yelled. Misaligned systems undermined everyone's progress and resolve. Once they realigned their compensation and performance evaluation systems to support the strategic goal, everyone could work together.

In Chapter 9—Respond with Regard—you got tools that emphasized the importance of reinforcing, celebrating, and rewarding courage and innovation. You get more of what you encourage and celebrate and less of what you ignore. Take a careful look at all aspects of your performance management and recognition systems. Do your performance appraisal process and tools rate and reward the behaviors you want to encourage? How about your approach to compensation? Who gets promoted and why? People will pay attention to what behaviors get rewarded far more than what you say is important.

John's executive team met and had a tough discussion about how each department would contribute to a successful product launch. They had to make hard decisions regarding current customer satisfaction and product development. Then they looked at how to align their incentive and reward programs to reinforce today's priorities.

David helped the team work through specific scenarios in which their reward and recognition systems seemed to be in conflict. They wrestled with how they would handle those situations in the future. In some cases, the answer was temporarily retooling their bonus structures. In others, the team decided they would need to have a "rapid response" meeting to discuss the issue.

You don't really know what's important until you've looked at what trade-offs you are and aren't willing to make. These weren't easy conversations. John finally leaned back and said, "No wonder you've been at each other's throats. If we're not clear about what we're doing, how can we expect our people to figure it out?"

MEASURING PROGRESS

Building culture takes time. You'll want to ensure you have good metrics in place to keep a pulse on the behaviors and outcomes you want to achieve. What does success look like in terms of behaviors at each level of your organization? What specific behaviors are most critical? How will you measure those (for example, the number of weekly one-on-ones, engagement surveys, exit interviews)? What are the short- and long-term outcomes you would hope to achieve (number of ideas; ratio of ideas generated to implemented; productivity improvements; customer retention; employee retention)?

FIRST TRACKS

Inventory Your Infrastructure

OBJECTIVES:
- To have a candid conversation about your infrastructure and support systems.
- To prioritize opportunities for greater alignment and support of the culture you're looking to build.

TIME REQUIRED:

About an hour.

PROCESS:

It may feel overwhelming to consider every part of your infrastructure at once. To get started, complete this quick audit of your infrastructure and systems. Each system gets two ratings. The first rating in Column A is a "Misalignment Index." (A rating of 10 is not aligned at all—it's creating the opposite of a Courageous Culture. A rating of 1 is very aligned.) The second rating in Column B is your level of influence. How much ability do you have to control, influence, or change this system? (A rating of 10 is 100 percent influence—I can change this today. A rating of 1 is 0 percent influence—for example, there's an external regulation or rule the entire company must work within.)

Once you've rated each item in both categories, multiply the numbers together. Each item will end up with a final score from 1 to 100.

SYSTEM	A MISALIGNMENT (1 LOW–10 HIGH)	B DEGREE OF INFLUENCE (1 LOW–10 HIGH)	FINAL SCORE (MULTIPLY A X B)
Recruiting			
Interviewing & Hiring			
Onboarding			
Compensation			
Recognition, Rewards, Bonus Structure			
Employee Training			
Performance Management			
Manager & Leadership Training			
Promotion & Succession Planning			

Items with a score of 70 or higher are candidates for immediate action. To keep it simple and build momentum, choose the highest-rated item and work with your team to build an action plan to address it.

CHAPTER 13

Managers Who Lead in Courageous Cultures

There's a world of difference between insisting on someone's doing something and establishing an atmosphere in
which that person can grow into wanting to do it.

—MR. ROGERS[1]

Throughout the book we've encouraged you and your leadership team to dance with Clarity and Curiosity as you start to build your Courageous Culture. If you've completed the First Tracks assignments with your team, you've created a strong foundation, and the people closest to your team have probably started to notice. Now it's time to take the next steps to build momentum and ensure your initial work gets traction.

We opened Courageous Cultures by describing the gap we often observe when executives think they're creating an open environment that encourages employees to speak up but are surprised to learn that employees are holding back. Even when you and your leadership team practice and encourage speaking up, problem solving, and advocating for customers, the success of your vision, strategy, and culture lives with your managers.

Each of the concepts and tools you've practiced with your team need to be translated and owned by the leaders and managers who have responsibility for people at every level of your organization.

Your employees experience your organization through their day-to-day team and their immediate leader. Amy Edmondson says it this way: "Psychological safety is experienced at a group level. People working together tend to have similar perceptions of whether or not the climate is psychologically safe."[2] People will not consistently speak up to solve problems or advocate for customers beyond what they feel is safe on their team. It's critical that you equip your leaders with the ability to build a Courageous Culture with their team.

This requires a consistent, intentional, and high-accountability approach to the culture on every team in your organization. It takes only a relatively small amount of toxic behavior to derail your efforts at building a Courageous Culture. Speaking about toxic employees at work, Wharton professor and bestselling author Adam Grant, says, "One bad apple can spoil a barrel, but one good egg does not make a dozen."[3] This should sound familiar. We discussed the way that negative memories can be stronger than memories of good experiences. This pattern of the negative having a stronger impact than the positive also holds true in finance where "losses have more of an impact than gains" and linguistics where "we pay more attention to negative words than positive ones."[4]

So how do you help your leaders at every level build a Courageous Culture filled with Microinnovators, Problem Solvers, and Customer Advocates? Equipping your managers to lead in a Courageous Culture is a microcosm of the work you've already done with your team, but viewed specifically through the lens of your managers' day-to-day work. To help your leaders at every level build a Courageous Culture, they'll need to experience the same journey you've taken—and you'll need to pay special attention to the infrastructure that supports (or hinders) their work.

WHY MANAGERS DON'T SUPPORT A COURAGEOUS CULTURE

It can be helpful to start with a look at what goes wrong when managers don't translate the Courageous Cultures Clarity-Curiosity Cycle to their teams. When we look at the breakdown between intentions and frontline experience, several common problems emerge.

1. Lack of Training

The number one reason people don't lead well is that they haven't been taught how. Despite the continual stream of findings about the difference that managers make for their teams,[5] most organizations don't equip people with the skills they need to be effective at leading and managing others.[6] If you don't have an intentional leadership development strategy, it's time to get one in place. If you already have a leadership development program, ensure that it's following best practices, including spaced learning over time (one-and-dones are usually a waste of time and money) and frequent application to real business issues.

FIVE WAYS TO LAUNCH A SUCCESSFUL LEADERSHIP DEVELOPMENT PROGRAM

Focus on Changing Behavior

What behaviors will change as a result of the program? How will this training ensure that you meet your strategic goals?

Include Participants' Managers

Hold a manager's briefing session before the program begins so that they understand the value to their team and their work, are prepared with strategic questions, and have a clear path to support their participants' learning and application. Include a manager's guide that makes it easy for them to engage with their participants and reinforce what their participants learn in the training.

Build in Sustained Learning Over Time

Your managers can't learn to lead in a single half-day workshop. Even if you have limited budget, find creative ways to build programs that combine learning with practice, reflection, and feedback. Be sure to include daily and weekly reinforcement of key behaviors.

Stir Up New Ideas and Critical Thinking to Improve the Business
Leadership development in a Courageous Culture doesn't just teach skills, it provides opportunities for application to improve the business. Work with a leadership development partner who will teach participants to think critically and creatively about their real business challenges and develop strategies to improve or solve them.

Support Managers' Reentry to Their Teams

No one likes to feel like an experiment as his manager, without any explanation, implements new ideas she's learned in training. Be sure the program includes a process for reentry—including a practical action plan for communicating what will be different, and why.

2. Insecurity

The second management-related killer of Courageous Cultures is insecurity. This was the challenge encountered by Peter, whom you met in Chapter 5. Despite his boss's boss, Joe, actively soliciting input, Peter's leader was insecure and feared that he would look bad and lose out if his team spoke the truth. This insecurity is incredibly common. We regularly hear from people who tell us that their immediate supervisors suppress information for fear that it will make them look bad.

Are these managers insecure because of unfounded fears? Or is their insecurity a rational response to conflicting expectations, senior leaders' sarcasm, and internal competition that prevents collaboration? When people doubt their footing, it's difficult for them to accept criticism, hear difficult truths, or be open to new ideas.

3. Conflicting Expectations and Accountability

Faced with getting results today, many managers don't know what to do with all the ideas that might come their way. They don't translate Courageous Culture intentions from senior leadership because their visible goals appear to conflict with having a team of people who speak up. As one manager told us, "What I need is for people to follow my directions. I know how this works. If they'll just do that, we'll make our targets." And perhaps they will—today. When managers take this approach, they're often focused on short-term success and can't see the long-term benefit of teams that solve problems, constantly improve, and take initiative to serve the customer.

Are these managers focused on short-term goals at the expense of long-term development and competitiveness because they're shortsighted and stubborn? Or is it because they know that making those targets is all that they are accountable to achieve? Intentions and suggestions alone won't change behaviors when there is strong accountability for transactional business results but no accountability for cultivating Curiosity.

HOW TO ENSURE YOUR MANAGERS CAN LEAD A COURAGEOUS CULTURE

The best way to help your managers lead a Courageous Culture is to have them experience it for themselves, align your infrastructure, training, and goals to support them, and then galvanize that work with consistent accountability. Let's take a look at how you can use the Clarity-Curiosity Cycle to develop your leaders.

Clarity: Fundamentals

Before they can get curious, ask credible courageous questions, or try out new ideas, your leaders need a solid foundation of leadership and management fundamentals. We address these essential skills in *Winning Well: A Manager's Guide to Getting Results Without Losing Your Soul.* A few of the most essential skills include:

- How to create a shared team vision of success.
- Establishing and reinforcing mutually understood expectations.
- Building trust and connection.
- Practicing drama-free accountability.
- Meetings that get results and that people want to attend.
- How to build employee confidence and competence.

With these fundamentals in place, your leaders and managers will be able to build on a foundation of trust and credibility as you help them experience the next part of the Courageous Cultures Cycle.

Curiosity: Experience a Courageous Culture

It's one thing to talk about speaking up, but there's no substitute for living it. As you and your team meet with managers, take them on the same journey you've experienced. You can use the First Tracks prompts—supplying the answers you've chosen and asking them to come up with their own, where appropriate. Additionally, your free, downloadable *Executive Strategy Guide* has many supplemental discussion questions you can use to facilitate these conversations.

In this phase of your manager's development, move beyond discussions, and practice the Courageous Culture skills you've been developing. Help them to Navigate the Narrative and tap into their own courage. Ask your managers the courageous questions you've identified and listen to their responses. If you don't feel like you're getting the truth, take a step back. Acknowledge the reticence in the room and reinforce that you really do want to get their perspective. When someone does speak up with a deeper insight or a potentially critical perspective, let them see you Respond with Regard. If it's been challenging to get people talking, celebrate it and invite more. Thank them for taking the initiative. Work with them to Practice the Principle and find the scalable ideas within best practices.

When it comes to building a Courageous Culture, lived experience makes all the difference. Ray Dalio, founder of the ultrasuccessful Bridgewater Associates hedge fund, describes how his expectation is that "no one has the right to hold a critical opinion without speaking up."[7] He made speaking up such an expected part of Bridgewater's culture that on one occasion, he received an email from Jim, an employee who'd attended a recent meeting that Ray led. The email read: "Ray, you deserve a 'D-minus' for your performance today in the meeting. . . . You did not prepare at all well because there is no way you could have been that disorganized."[8] Jim went on to request that Ray come more prepared and even offered to help him warm up before the meeting began. That may be more directly worded than you'd want in your culture, but how would you respond? Ray responded by celebrating the feedback, sharing it with everyone in the company, and then sharing it with an entire TED audience and the millions who would later watch it. That's the difference between talking about it and experiencing it.

Another way you can overcome a manager's insecurity and normalize risk and recovery is to occasionally share a story of a leadership mistake you made and how you learned from it. We were working with Drew, an incredibly conscientious senior leader at a construction design firm, and a team of seasoned and emerging leaders. Reflecting on his decades of leadership, he told us and his colleagues, "I don't think I told everyone often enough that I make mistakes." The price of not sharing mistakes, he explained, was that people didn't feel safe to make their own, nor could they get the benefit of what he'd already learned from his mistakes.

Finally, here is a technique to help your play-it-safe managers. Teach your reluctant leaders to generate and answer a list of questions that helps them have a more open mind. Such as:

- What's driving your hesitation?
- Who else needs to be involved to make you feel comfortable?
- What do you think would happen if we implemented this?

As they explore the answers, they'll often discover that the downside was not as scary as they assumed. Show them that it's okay to be wrong when taking action—and be sure that's true. Then, help them move through their hesitation to implementation. One major cause of decision paralysis is that it feels so permanent. Find a way to let them taste the results of a decision in a way that can be easily reversed. Got a new process? Try it with one team. Worried about the customer experience? Try your idea out with a small subset of customers and carefully monitor the experience. It's a lot easier to try a pilot program than to convince a risk-averse decision-maker to make a "permanent" change, and you've helped them experience Respond with Regard and Practice the Principle.

Clarity: Clarify Roles, Expectations, and Accountability

Once you've equipped your managers with fundamental skills and invited them to participate in Courageous Culture with you, it's time to clarify expectations. Return to your why: Why are you investing in a Courageous Culture? Share your personal vision of how teams of Microinnovators, Problem Solvers, and Customer Advocates are vital for a competitive future. Ensure that your managers know that they are expected to create the same environment that they've experienced with you. Don't assume that this is understood. Be clear that you expect your leaders at every level to build cultures of consistent contribution, to Navigate the Narrative, Cultivate Curiosity, Respond with Regard, Practice the Principle, and Galvanize the Genius. The easiest place for them to start is by replicating what you've done with them: sharing mistakes to build trust and shorten learning curves, asking courageous questions, then receiving and responding to feedback, solutions, and ideas that better serve the customers.

As managers receive projects and assignments, give them the Clarity that makes Curiosity possible. When we spoke with Basecamp cofounder Jason Fried, he described this process as autonomy and agency. "We assign projects," he explained, "where the boundaries are clearly staked out. The details are up to the team. When you say, 'Here are the boundaries, what can you do within them?'—that's how you build your team's thinking and problem solving."

Curiosity: Creative Development

You've committed to develop your managers and ensure everyone has a solid foundation of leadership training. They know what's expected of them and have experienced some basics of leading in a Courageous Culture—now what? Our clients often ask us to help them take their leadership developmental plans to the next level. Check out the sidebar for a few of our favorite ideas. We would love to hear your ideas as well.

CREATIVE LEADERSHIP DEVELOPMENT

1. DIY (Do-It-Yourself) 360-Degree Feedback

Formal 360-degree feedback assessments are a great way to get structured, anonymous feedback from teams, peers, and leaders. We're big fans. But the truth is, what makes these tools valuable is the conversation that follows. If a formal 360-degree feedback tool is not available or practical, you can achieve similar results by helping them conduct a DIY 360. In fact, a personal conversation where a manager tells her team members and colleagues that she's working to be more effective in a specific area (meetings, communication, supporting staff development), and asks for feedback, helps her develop, but it also reinforces a Courageous Culture. You'll find a step-by-step guide to help your managers conduct their DIY 360 in your *Executive Strategy Guide*.

2. Interdepartment Field Trips

There's a reason why almost every elementary school takes a trip to the zoo. You can read about giraffes all you want, but until you have one bend down and lick your face, it's hard to understand just how challenging it is to go through life with a neck like that. Help managers arrange a visit to meet with their peers in another department or shadow them to learn more about their roles. It's always amazing to see how quickly such visits increase understanding and trust.

3. Action Learning Projects

When done well, "action learning projects" are incredible ways to learn while working on improving the business, as well as giving your managers exposure to the executive team. You provide a small group of managers with a business challenge, success criteria, and a sponsor. They work together to complete the project and then present their outcomes to members of your executive team.

4. Book Groups

Read a leadership book as a team. You can use your *Executive Strategy Guide* and the First Tracks assignments to guide a discussion (or equip another leader to facilitate—and help them grow in the process).

5. Author a LinkedIn Article

Encourage your employees to come up with a teachable point of view on LinkedIn and write an article. This is a great way to help them think critically and to work on building their professional brand. Note: Some companies have PR guidelines around this, but most companies are okay with employees posting their thoughts about leadership or industry expertise if they stay away from using the company name or proprietary information.

6. Speak at an Industry Conference

There are so many benefits to preparing for and delivering a breakout session at an industry conference—the research, the delivery prep, the presentation, feedback, and of course the benchmarking comparisons with competitors—not to mention the benefits of attending the conference itself.

Clarity: Galvanize the Genius

When leaders embark on culture change, it's easy for great intentions and training to get lost in the press of day-to-day work. One of the most important roles you can play to help your managers build a Courageous Culture is to prevent the corrosive, slow slide back to the way things were. In Chapter 11 we gave you the tools to Galvanize the Genius and ensure that new behaviors got traction. You use the same process to reinforce culture. The final element to helping your managers lead in a Courageous Culture is accountability.

There are many ways to indirectly assess how your managers are leading, but there's no substitute for direct observation. How can you watch your leaders in action? Perhaps you attend a meeting they're running, visit with their team in a skip-level conversation, or make a site visit to watch their team in action. Have them discuss their 360-degree feedback with you. You might ask about:

- The last great idea they heard from their team.
- The last courageous question they asked their team.
- The last mistake they made and what they learned from it.
- What best practice they have contributed to their colleagues in the past two months.

With one visit and a few questions, you can find many Courageous Culture outcomes to celebrate and reinforce. You'll quickly get a sense of whether they're building an environment of speaking up, microinnovation, and customer advocacy. When that happens, work with their supervisor and clarify your leadership expectations while getting curious about why it's not happening. You may discover another unaligned infrastructure issue that you can address—or you might learn that they're not comfortable leading in this culture. Either way, the manager, the team, and your organization come out ahead.

FIRST TRACKS

Manager Development Plan

OBJECTIVES:

- To build an intentional approach to prepare your managers for leading in a Courageous Culture.

TIME REQUIRED:

Sixty to ninety minutes.

PROCESS:

1. Review your existing management training. Do your managers receive instruction and reinforcement in critical leadership and management skills before they are placed in roles with responsibility for people? If not, how will you address this gap?

2. How and when will you communicate with your managers your personal vision regarding the importance of a Courageous Culture and teams of Microinnovators, Problem Solvers, and Customer Advocates?

3. Where and when will you invite managers to participate in your Courageous Cultures journey (for example, Navigate the

Narrative, participate in a Fear Forage, answer and ask coura-geous questions, solicit direct feedback, and model positive response)?

4. How and when will you communicate Courageous Culture leadership and management expectations? What is one activity you will give your managers to begin their practice? (For example, at your next meeting, ask a courageous question related to your current top goal. Or at your next meeting tell your team a two-to-three-minute story of a mistake you made, what you learned from it, and what you hope they're able to take away from your mistake.)

5. When and how will you follow up to Galvanize the Genius and ensure that your managers are implementing Courageous Culture behaviors in their teams?

CHAPTER 14

People Are Different:
How to Leverage Your Diverse
Talent to Build a Courageous Culture

Imperfections are not inadequacies; they are reminders that
we're all in this together.

—BRENÉ BROWN, *The Gifts of Imperfection*[1]

We gathered in a conference room where we'd been invited to
conduct a long-term leadership development program with
fifteen talented engineers, designers, and project managers.
In many ways, they fit the image you might have when you think of
a room of engineers. Most were quiet and analytical. They chose
their words carefully. They worked hard to be right. But if you'd
judged the creativity and passion in the room by the personality of
the people sitting around the conference table, you might have
missed the tremendous energy bubbling below.

As we laid the foundation for Courageous Cultures, we asked
them to reflect on "why you do what you do" and share their
thoughts with the group. When it was time for Greg, one of the
firm's senior leaders, to speak, he looked down at his notes. "I love
this work. We start with a blank piece of paper and then . . ." He
looked up from his notes and his eyes shone with passion. "We create something. From nothing. And that's amazing."

People smiled in agreement. And then one of the quietest managers chimed in about how "freakin' cool" it is to take an idea someone imagined and conjure it into existence. A designer caught his eye and added, "And it's so real that the hospital we just created will still be there in fifty years. *We made that.* Thousands of patients will go through there. And how we built it matters."

WHO'S ON YOUR TEAM?

If you're like many leaders with whom we've shared Courageous Cultures, you're mentally indexing your team and wondering if they're capable of microinnovations, problem solving, and advocating for your customer. You might be thinking about the "idea machines" who present countless ideas, none of them quite relevant to your business. Or maybe you worry about the people who seem to have a "tell me what to do" attitude. Can they make it in a Courageous Culture? Some leaders look at their people, shake their heads, and say, "They can't get there from here." Sometimes that's true. But often it isn't. If you're serious about building a true Courageous Culture, before encouraging them to opt out and find another job, we invite you to pause and think about how you can adopt your strategy for more opt-ins to help them engage and contribute.

Yes, people come with a wide variety of passions, perspectives, and personalities. Courageous Cultures leverage all that diverse talent. But sometimes, like with those quiet engineers, it's easy to make assumptions and miss people's energy and potential. There are quieter voices you can amplify and embryonic ideas to nurture. We believe that most people can participate in a Courageous Culture, but it doesn't happen without real effort from you and your leaders.

Recruiting talent that will thrive and contribute to a Courageous Culture is part of the solution (as we discussed in Chapter 12), but it's not the only answer. In fact, if you focus too much on recruiting for people who will speak up, you can end up with combative teams that don't listen to one another or think through problems. And teams of rock star innovators are too much without some people who will continue to ask, "How do we operationalize this?" Leading a Courageous Culture requires you and your leadership team to bring together different people and blend their talents in the dance between Clarity and Curiosity. In our conversation with Nestlé's Sonia Studer, she explained how Nestlé prizes diversity because it allows them to "better understand and anticipate the needs of our consumers—something that is key to our success as a company." Genuine teams of Microinnovators, Problem Solvers, and Customer Advocates start by bringing together diverse talent.

How do you work with diverse talent in a Courageous Culture?

Start by recognizing the differences. Too many leaders aren't able to cultivate the courage they want because they don't recognize the normal differences in their people. This creates many conflicts and violates people's expectations. Here are a few examples:

- Maria gives the team the freedom she craves from her own manager, but it confuses her team full of people who prefer more daily attention, and they feel like Maria doesn't care about them.
- Dale methodically adds the new project his manager gave him to the bottom of his to-do list. But he frustrates his manager who thought Dale would intuitively understand that this project trumps everything and needs to be done right away.
- Dion comes to a staff meeting prepared to take part, arrives early, sits in front, and his teammate, Jill, thinks he's angry because he didn't engage or talk with anyone while the meeting was getting ready to start.
- Laura, a database manager, works long hours to ensure the data is accurate and then quits when Kathy, her team leader, ignores her data in favor of political relationships.

At their core, all these relationship breakdowns happened because the leader didn't understand that people are different. When it comes to building a Courageous Culture, one of the fundamental differences is a person's preference for process or creation. People who prefer to manage process have a strong preference for Clarity. Those who prefer to create have a strong preference for Curiosity. Part of building and maintaining a Courageous Culture is to bring these folks together and leverage their natural strengths while helping them navigate the dance between Clarity and Curiosity.

There are many tools available to familiarize you and your team with the basics of work-related human diversity. The specific tool is not as important as the fundamental understanding that people are different, that these differences can add value, and that you need to figure out the best ways to leverage the strengths of the human beings on your team. No one wants to be just tolerated. Leading a Courageous Culture requires you and your leaders to intentionally seek out different perspectives, backgrounds, experiences, and ways of thinking. You'll do your best for your customers when leaders value every person for the meaningful contribution they make. As you leverage diverse talent, your employees learn to emulate that behavior when working with a wide range of (sometimes frustrating) customers.

Next, give people what they need to be effective in a Courageous Culture. As your leaders learn how their people are wired and what energizes them, they can meet them where they are to draw greatness from them. Let's look at several types of people that present a challenge for leaders who want to build Courageous Cultures.

Silent Wounded

They don't trust you—and with good reason. It's not that you've done anything wrong. The three managers they had before this job abused their trust, told them they weren't hired to think, stole their idea, then took credit for it. Now you have the same title and, fairly or not, all the baggage that comes with it.

Your number one leadership job with the silent wounded is to rebuild their trust. This will take time, but once you've built that trust, these team members are often very loyal. Start small. Ask an almost-courageous question and receive the answers graciously, with gratitude. Build up to deeper questions and Respond with Regard as the answers are more vulnerable. Celebrate people, generously give credit, then ask for more problem solving and ideas to better serve your customers.

Once you've established a bit of a track record, you may need to have a conversation with some of the silent wounded who cling to their scars ("I'm wondering if I've done anything to violate your trust? Can we move forward together?").

When Karin worked with her sales team to transform morale and shift to small business sales, she had a few silent wounded in the mix. It took time—and she lost one along the way. (As her team describes it, he fired her as he moved to another department.) But the most fulfilling transformation was watching trust build over time with the biggest naysayers, as they became masters of the Clarity-Curiosity dance and built those competencies in their team.

Silent Ponderous

We were discussing Courageous Cultures with the CEO of a talent development company and she paused, looked thoughtful, and then told us about one of her reluctant team members.

> He didn't contribute many ideas, but it wasn't because he was afraid. It took me a while to understand that he was being thoughtful. He wanted to figure out if the idea was valuable and work through the details before he shared it. I learned that if I wanted his most innovative ideas, I had to find ways to slow down the conversation, even as we were moving fast.

These silent ponderous types are often quiet introverts, and it can be hard to tell what they are thinking or feeling. If you're an expressive, gung-ho type who calls every team member into the conversation and genuinely wants their opinion, it can be frustrating when they don't dive in with you. They can also get frustrated because by the time they've determined what they think about the topic, the conversation has often moved on.

To draw out the great value silent, ponderous people can contribute, start by giving them time to think. For some meetings, this means giving them the main topic a day or two in advance and asking them to think about it. In some settings, simply having everyone write down ideas first will give everyone time to process. Another strategy that can help is to make it clear that you're not asking for a fully-thought-through, 100 percent accurate answer. Sometimes the silent, ponderous people won't answer because they don't want to be wrong. When you ask them for their best thinking in this moment, or for a range of ideas, it gives them permission to explore rather than making them feel as though they must commit to a "right" idea.

Just-Do-What-I-Sayers or Let-Me-Do-My-Thing-ers

You may have leaders or individual contributors who are certain of their direction and methods. These leaders are often successful and just want people to line up behind them and do what they're told. Individual contributors with this characteristic may be high performers but have difficulty teaming with other people.

When you talk with people in this group, it may be challenging. After all, they're good and they know it. They've done well. It can help to frame the conversation in terms of their goals. If they want to have more responsibility or more influence, those are easy opportunities to talk about the people skills they need to practice and demonstrate. If they want to improve their outcomes, they'll need people and their ideas. Two points you can emphasize in these conversations are: (1) Success in this organization is everyone thinking and contributing. (2) You care about their career and want them to succeed—and that's why you're having this conversation.

Another strategy that can help your let-me-do-my-thing high performers is to reframe "their thing." Ask them to consider courageous questions like:

- What's ticking off or delighting your customers?
- What frustrates or energizes your team?
- What's freaking out or motivating your boss?
- Why are your peers so demoralized?

Once they've identified the pain points or motivators, have them look for little ways to make life better for their customers and colleagues. What process can they improve? What problem can they solve? For some people in this group, just the act of looking at these questions shifts their perspective and realigns their leadership.

Just-Tell-Me-What-to-Do-ers

There are a couple types of people who consistently just want to be told what to do. The first group are the silent wounded described above who seek safety by just following directions. They have often been frustrated by leaders who asked for their opinion and then criticized, rejected, or even punished them for their perspective. They have a "you won't fool me again" mantra. As with other silent wounded, take time to rebuild trust with small steps that prove you mean what you say.

The second group of people who want you to "just tell me what to do" are doing what they know has made them successful in the past. Through much of school and in many organizations, you can get along quite well by just following instructions. Often, they were hired for this same characteristic. The challenge for these people is the same as for organizations everywhere: the world is changing and computers are far more efficient at being told what to do.

For this group, there are three steps you can take. First, have a discussion about the changing nature of work and what it will take for your business to thrive. Next, reframe what success looks like for their role. In effect, you are still answering their need to "be told what to do" but in a way that asks them to consider the opportunities and problems facing the organization. Finally, equip them with the ability to contribute ideas.

As we shared in Chapter 3, 40 percent of people surveyed said they don't feel confident to share their ideas and 45 percent say they haven't been trained to think critically or solve problems. These are both common challenges shared by just-tell-me-what-to-do-ers. Here are two of our favorite techniques to address both challenges.

Help them Share an IDEA

If you want better ideas, help your employees know what differentiates a good IDEA by giving them a few criteria to follow. When they can think through these elements, their idea has a better chance of being used and making a difference.

- **I—Interesting.** Why is this idea interesting? What strategic problem does it solve? How will results be made better by this idea (customer experience, employee retention, efficiency)?
- **D—Doable.** Is this idea something we could actually do? How would we make it happen? What would make it easier or more difficult?
- **E—Engaging.** Who would we need to engage to make this happen? Why should they support it? Where are we most likely to meet resistance?
- **A—Actions.** What are the most important actions needed to try this? How would we start?

TEAM *SHARK TANK*™–STYLED COMPETITIONS

One of the best ways to develop this confidence is practice. If your employees struggle with innovation and problem solving, you can use the IDEA framework where all team members bring their best idea to pitch. Facilitate a *Shark Tank*–type competition as the teams hear, discuss, and vote on one another's ideas.

Nine "Whats" Business Coaching

Another way to help your just-tell-me-what-to-do-ers is to develop their critical thinking and ability to solve problems. There's a certain rush from jumping in and doing what must be done at exactly the right time. It might feel good, but it's the easiest way to sabotage long-term success. When you solve problems *for* your team instead of *with* your team, you teach them to stop thinking. Take time to slow down just enough, even during times of crisis, to bring others along and help them rise to the occasion. Don't be a hero, be a hero farmer.

When they don't know how to solve a problem, the management cliché of "Don't bring me a problem without a solution" means your team won't bring you problems. The following Nine "Whats" coaching questions will help you to free up your own time and increase your team's ability to think and problem solve on their own.

1. *What is your goal?* Start here to check for understanding and ensure that the team member has a good grasp of the task and is focused on the right goal.
2. *What have you tried?* This question ensures you don't spend time covering ground already explored. It also requires your team member to make some effort before requesting help.
3. *What happened?* Finish gathering facts by asking about the consequences of the solutions already tried. Sometimes just the act of talking about it will help the team member find a new solution.

4. *What did you learn from this?* With this question, you ask team members to reflect on their experience. Often, the act of examining what happened and what learning they can draw from it will spark a new approach.

5. *What else do you need?* This is a check to see if there is additional training or equipment needed. Sometimes your team members will say something like: "You know, if I knew how to use pivot tables, I think I could do this." Great—connect them to a spreadsheet guru for a quick lesson and get them moving.

6. *What else can you do?* Now it's time to have them generate some new options. When you ask this question, you'll usually hear one of two answers. Either your team members will say, "I don't know," or will offer some options: "Well, I was thinking I could try option A or I could try option B." If she says, "I don't know," we'll come back to that with question nine. Let's assume for now that she offers some options.

7. *What do you think will happen if you try option A? What about option B?* You're asking your team members to explore the potential consequences of their proposed solution. This gives you insight into their thinking and helps them think through what makes their choices viable or desirable.

   If they are missing a critical piece of information, you can supply it here without telling them what to do: "One additional factor you will want to know is that the customer considers that a vital feature."

8. *What will you do?* This is the critical step that you've been leading up to. As you helped them review the facts, reflect on what they learned, explore alternatives, and the consequences of each choice, the goal is for your team members to choose their solution.

   When they choose it, they own it. If they choose something that seems to be a clearly inferior option, you can ask them to help you understand why they think that's their best option. If they don't understand some of the other issues affecting the decision, you can also add those to the mix.

9. *The Ninth What.* You might be wondering what to do if the person replies to one of your questions with "I don't know." "I don't know" can mean many things. Rarely does it mean the person has zero thoughts about the issue. More often, "I don't know" translates to:

"I'm uncertain."
"I don't want to commit before I know where you stand."
"I haven't thought about it yet."
"Will you please just tell me what to do?"
"I'm scared about getting it wrong."

Your job as a leader is to continue the dialogue—to ease the person through his anxiety. When someone says, "I don't know," your ninth question is: "What might you do if you did know?" The person who was stymied two seconds ago will start to share ideas, brainstorm solutions, and move on as if they were never stuck. It's amazing and hard to believe until you try it.

This question works because it addresses the source of the person's "I don't know." If she was anxious or fearful, it takes the pressure off with tentative language: "If you did know . . ." Now your team member doesn't have to be certain or look for your approval and she's free to share whatever she might have been thinking.

If the person hadn't thought about the issue or didn't want to think about it, you've lowered the perceived amount of energy he has to spend. You're not asking for a thesis on the subject, just a conversational "What might you do?"

Our brains can do amazing work when we remove the emotional blocks. When you do this for your team, you train their brain to engage, to push through their ordinary blocks, and increase their performance. Ultimately, they will be able to have these conversations with themselves and will need to bring only the very serious issues to you.

You've just increased your team's capacity for problem solving, freed up time to focus on your work, and . . . you've built a leader!

IDEA GRENADIERS

Some people are idea machines—their brains work overtime to see the possibilities in every situation. Nearly every team is better off with someone who can creatively look at what's happening and see opportunities to improve or transform. The challenge comes when the idea person starts tossing all his ideas in your lap, wants you to do them, but won't do the work. These are the "idea grenadiers"— tossing ideas like grenades and then running in the other direction.

When you're working with people like this, it helps to have a direct conversation that calls them back to what matters most and asks them to engage. For example:

> I've noticed that in the past month you've come to me with four different ideas about how we should improve security, re-vamp the training program, change our workforce manage-ment, and reorganize product management. There is merit in your ideas—and we can't pursue all of them right now. Which of them do you think would help achieve our number one stra-tegic priority? Is that a project you'd be willing to help with?

CREATORS

With a strong preference for the Curiosity phase of the Courageous Cultures Cycle, your creators love doing what they see as the "real work"—building new products and services. They're usually impa-tient with process and hate paperwork. Creators often resist cul-tural efforts to establish Clarity and label these efforts as oppressive, stifling, or limiting.

David met Russ, a senior program manager at a Bay Area soft-ware company, who was part of a grassroots team doing work to help his company navigate the Clarity-Curiosity dance. Russ ex-plained how he and his team have worked with their creators to help them incorporate Clarity processes:

We have a tradition of creativity—we really value it. For us, it's all about riding that line between creativity and Clarity. We've got teams that move very quickly and customers asking for all kinds of new work, and we say, "Yes, we can do all that amazing and cool work." But there's a massive need for us to be able to deliver quality product. The process to drive quality can be frustrating. When we introduce a new framework to ensure quality, instead of asking creative questions and what we could do that is cool, fancy, and shiny, you have to spend time thinking about the framework and how to use it. At first, that is frustrating, but—and this has made the difference—as people get used to the framework, they don't have to think about it anymore and they can be even more creative.

It's burdensome in the moment because you have to think about it, but then it becomes second nature and part of your culture. When you drive, you're not constantly thinking, "I've got to turn on my turn signal," right? When you turn, you shift down, and turn on the signal, then you make your turn. It's just done and you're already thinking about a mile ahead and where you're going. As people have experienced these quality frameworks, they've realized that the little bit of work now is saving effort down the road and is helping us be more creative, faster.

SCHMOOZERS

Most organizations have a schmoozer—whom everyone likes and who talks a great game, but when it comes time to get things done, somehow, the schmoozers never implement that plan that sounded so amazing when they presented it. The challenge with schmoozers in a Courageous Culture is that they undermine trust. The ideas they share lack credibility and they're less likely to be entrusted with good ideas because they won't implement them.

The best strategy with schmoozers is to ignore the charm and focus on the results. Conversations that focus on accountability and that help them raise their game will help restore their credibility. When you talk with them, be ready for an elegantly worded explanation for why they didn't get it done. If it happens again, you need to escalate the conversation. For example: "This is the third time we've had this conversation. Right now, your credibility is at stake. What you said sounded wonderful, but if you can't implement it, your team can't rely on you and neither can I. What can we do to get this on track and completed?"

OXYGEN SUCKERS

The next challenging type are those who suck all the air out of the room. They often talk so much, so loud, or so vehemently that others don't have a chance to contribute. Oxygen suckers can spark drama that derails a healthy conversation and wastes time on tangents. Oxygen suckers often lack self-awareness and don't recognize how their behavior affects others. It's up to you to facilitate in a way that manages everyone's time to speak.

To help your oxygen suckers, start with a direct conversation. Privately explain that you are going to run meetings differently and that your goal is to make sure everyone participates equitably. Be specific about how you'll do this. For example: "In some cases I will time people's comments to ensure everyone gets a chance to speak. I may ask you to speak after I've asked some of the quieter team members for their perspective."

CHANGE RESISTORS

Finally, there are the change resistors. You're energized about a new solution or strategy, but your enthusiasm is met with quiet reluctance. Then your team brings up three different operational challenges and two reasons your customers won't like it. Why can't they understand the benefit and just move forward? The resistance to change frustrates many leaders, but it doesn't have to. In fact, the resistance you feel often means there's an opportunity to Cultivate Curiosity and create buy-in.

Your change resistors aren't necessarily lazy, stuck, negative, or even "resistant." Rather, they're normal. Resisting change actually makes a lot of sense. After all, if what you did yesterday worked—it got you through the day alive, fed, and healthy—why spend energy to do something differently? That's a waste of time—unless there's a good reason. To address this, start with the problem, not the solution. When you start with the solution, you deprive your team of the understanding and connection that drove you to action.

Share the problem, then pause. Let it sink in. Then ask for their thoughts. This helps anchor the problem in their thinking. They explore the consequences and how it interacts with other issues. Change always starts with desire or dissatisfaction. By introducing the problem and letting it sink in, you're creating the same emotional connection that moved you. As the team discusses the issue, they are likely to start asking about solutions. When someone asks you, "What do you think we should do?" resist the urge to answer immediately. Instead, continue to ask for their ideas. They may come up with ideas you haven't considered—or they may arrive at the same solution you've thought through. Either way, you've Cultivated Curiosity, created ownership, and built momentum.

It may feel like this process takes extra time—and it does. But it's fifteen or thirty minutes of time that prevents days, weeks, and even months of procrastination and foot-dragging. The team owns the problem and the solution. They've connected to the why and are ready for action. This small investment of time overcomes some common reasons people resist change.

A couple of notes:

- If you suspect an individual is resisting because they will lose something (status, money, comfort) you will need to address that separately. Maybe there is a bigger why available that makes the trade-off worth it. Or it may be an unavoidable consequence of a changing world. Don't overlook these personal losses—they are real and, if left unaddressed, make you look inhuman.

- Sometimes you need to move quickly. The more you connect with your team and connect them to the why behind the change, the more buy-in you'll have for the times you need to say, "Trust me and we'll discuss it later."

With all of these challenging types, your approach and the conversations give them a chance to participate in a Courageous Culture. Some people will choose not to—and that's okay. If people tell you that they can't perform at the level that's needed or they don't want to adjust their style, thank them for their honesty, honor their choice, and help them with their exit strategy.

FIRST TRACKS

Courageous Cultures Team Inventory

OBJECTIVES:
- To reflect on all members of your team and how you can best leverage their strengths and opportunities for growth.
- To identify gaps where you have opportunities to fill with future staffing.

TIME REQUIRED:
Thirty to sixty minutes, depending on the size of your team.

PROCESS:
As you think about leveraging your diverse talent to build a Courageous Culture, it's helpful to look at your team as a whole. The Courageous Cultures Team Inventory will help you visualize where you have strengths and where you will have to work harder to develop a core competency.

As you consider the people on your team, plot them on the following graph. To find their positions, consider how you would rate them on each axis of Clarity and Curiosity. Then, use the graph in Figure 14-1 and place a dot at the intersection of the axes. Repeat the process for each team member.

When thinking of their Clarity, consider the following scale:

1—No demonstrated understanding of what matters most, no focus on critical success behaviors, little to no team accountability.

10—Laser-like focus on what success looks like, understands and communicates critical success behaviors, diligently holds team accountable.

When thinking of their Curiosity, consider the following scale:

1—Ignores problems or passes them to others. Does not contribute ideas that will improve the team or better serve the customer.

10—Continually explores ways to improve the organization, solve problems, and better serve the customer. Asks insightful questions and frequently contributes relevant, meaningful ideas.

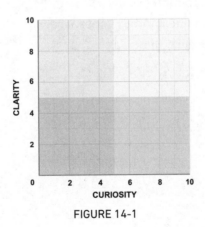

FIGURE 14-1

Once you've plotted your team on the graph, look at the pattern that emerges. First, let's look at two patterns that lend themselves to Courageous Cultures:

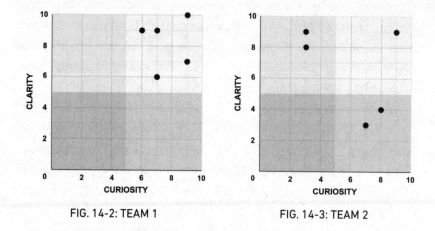

FIG. 14-2: TEAM 1   FIG. 14-3: TEAM 2

Clarity and Curiosity are present in both of these teams. Team 1's members are balanced and alternate very easily between both aspects. Team 2 has individuals with a strong Clarity focus and others with a strong Curiosity focus. This team has the elements of a successful Courageous Culture if both elements are brought together and you help the team leverage both strengths in turn. It will probably require some intentional effort to help your team members see the value in one another's approach.

If your plot looks like these . . .

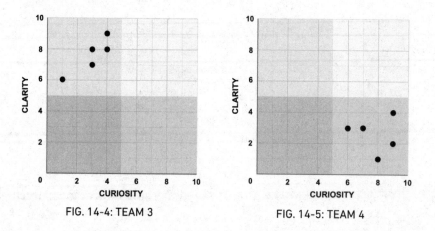

FIG. 14-4: TEAM 3   FIG. 14-5: TEAM 4

. . . you will want to focus on developing the focus that doesn't come as easily for your team. You can model it, you can coach to it using the techniques in this book, or you can hire for it.

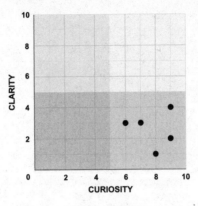

FIG. 14-6: TEAM 5

When your team looks like Team 5, focus on development. Start with Clarity (see your First Tracks from Chapter 7). Once that foundation is in place, you can begin to Cultivate Curiosity (with your First Tracks from Chapter 8).

Now that you've plotted your team, what will you do to help them function in the upper right quadrant with both Clarity and Curiosity?

To schedule a full Courageous Cultures assessment of your team or organization, please contact us at info@letsgrowleaders.com.

CHAPTER 15

Your Courageous Future

I believe that the most important single thing, beyond disci-
pline and creativity . . . is daring to dare.

— MAYA ANGELOU[1]

When we come home after a run of Courageous Cultures programs, we love to sit by the fire and carefully read and reflect on the hundreds of handwritten notes in which participants share their most courageous act at work.

The moments are filled with pride and hope, of human beings connecting with their values and taking a stand. Before you finish this book, we hope you will take a moment to reflect on your own courage map and remember your moments of courage and why they matter.

Of course, in every stack of notes, there are invariably the stories that make us well up with tears or visceral anger. These are the stories of human beings dealing with serious soul-sucking, toxic behaviors—that no one should have to face in our workplaces, churches, nonprofits, government agencies, or homes. The common denominator in these moments of courage? People felt remarkably alone.

Courage is often portrayed as a lonely act—taking a stand when no one else will; being the first to speak truth to power; being the only one to do what they said couldn't be done.

Courage doesn't have to be lonely. In fact, it's less effective when it is.

At times on this journey you will feel incredibly lonely. When you do, don't wear that as a badge of honor—instead find the others. They're out there, we promise. We talk to them every day in every single organization we work with. They're doing powerful and important work. And you can too, by waking up every day and dancing with Clarity and Curiosity and "daring to dare."

When you surround yourself with others who also believe that silence isn't safe and that effort is everything, you'll soon find you feel lonelier hiding your truth than speaking it. Don't forget that your team is watching too. When you advocate for them and your customers, they'll feel that they're in good company when they do too. And just like that, you have others acting courageously and doing what must be done, while encouraging one another. That's the paradox of a truly Courageous Culture: the more courage in your culture, the less courage you ask from individuals.

Your first tracks on this journey will likely be the most difficult, as well as the most rewarding. As you find the others, those lonely footprints will begin to form into a well-laid path of courage and hope for others to follow. That's the power of a Courageous Culture.

Courageous Cultures

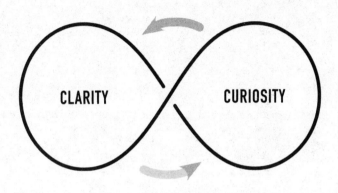

FIG. 15-1

1. **Navigate the Narrative.** Leverage your courageous moments to inspire future confidence.
2. **Create Clarity.** Build a foundation of safety, direction, and confidence.
3. **Cultivate Curiosity.** Intentionally seek out ideas, engagement, and solutions.
4. **Respond with Regard.** Acknowledge, celebrate, and invite more contribution.
5. **Practice the Principle.** Find the universal ideas that can scale and localize best practices.
6. **Galvanize the Genius.** Build momentum, sustain success, and prevent a return to old behaviors.
7. **Build an Infrastructure for Courage.** Align system and processes to support your Courageous Culture.

Notes

Foreword

1. Robert I. Sutton, "Some Bosses Live in a Fool's Paradise," *Harvard Business Review*, June 3, 2010. Accessed at https://hbr.org/2010/06/some-bosses-live -in-a-fools-pa.
2. C. F. Bond Jr. and E. L. Anderson, "The Reluctance to Transmit Bad News: Private Discomfort or Public Display?" *Journal of Experimental Social Psychology*, 23 (1987), pp. 176–187.
3. See Chapter 2 in A. C. Edmondson, *The Fearless Organization: Creating Psychological Safety for Learning, Innovation and Growth* (New York: Wiley, 2019).
4. A.C. Edmondson, "Psychological Safety and Learning Behavior in Work Teams," *Administrative Science Quarterly*, 44(4) (1999): pp. 350–383.
5. Edmondson, "Psychological Safety and Learning Behavior in Work Teams," pp. 350–383.
6. Edmondson, "Psychological Safety and Learning Behavior in Work Teams," pp. 350–383.
7. See Chapter 7 in A. C. Edmondson, *The Fearless Organization*.

Chapter 1

1. Seth Godin, "People Like Us Do Stuff Like This," *Seth's Blog*. Accessed October 27, 2019 at https://seths.blog/2013/07/people-like-us-do-stuff-like-this/.
2. We have changed the names of these leaders.

Chapter 2

1. Steve Blank, "Why Companies Do 'Innovation Theater' Instead of Actual Innovation, *Harvard Business Review*, October 7, 2019. Accessed at https://hbr.org/2019/10/why-companies-do-innovation-theater-instead-of-actual-innovation.

2. Aaron Smith and Janna Anderson, "AI, Robotics, and the Future of Jobs," Pew Research Center, August 6, 2014. Accessed September 15, 2019, at http://www.pewinternet.org/2014/08/06/future-of-jobs/.

3. Jennifer Liu, "AI Is Changing How Much Workers Trust Their Managers—and That Could Be a Good Thing," CNBC, October 15, 2019. Accessed at https://www.cnbc.com/2019/10/15/ai-is-changing-how-much-workers-trust-their-managerswhy-thats-good.html.

4. "US Business Leadership in the World in 2017," PriceWaterhouseCoopers. Accessed June 10, 2019, at https://www.pwc.com/gx/en/ceo-survey/pdf/20th-global-ceo-survey-us-supplement-executive-dialogues.pdf.

5. "How Many Gig Workers Are There?" Gig Economy Data Hub. Accessed October 1, 2019, at https://www.gigeconomydata.org/basics/how-many-gig-workers-are-there.

6. Entrepreneur Staff, "41 Percent of Generation Z-ers Plan to Be Entrepreneurs (Infographic)," *Entrepreneur*. Accessed August 23, 2019, at https://www.entrepreneur.com/article/326354.

Chapter 3

1. T. S. Eliot, "The Love Song of J. Alfred Prufrock," from *Collected Poems 1909–1962* (1963). Accessed January 6, 2020, at https://www.poetryfoundation.org/poetrymagazine/poems/44212/the-love-song-of-j-alfred-prufrock.

2. Amy Edmondson, *The Fearless Organization* (Hoboken, NJ: Wiley, 2019), p. 118.

3. Edmondson, *The Fearless Organization*, p. 32.

4. Edmondson, *The Fearless Organization*, p. 4.

5. Khalil Smith, Chris Weller, and David Rock, "Create a Workplace Where Everyone Feels Comfortable Speaking Up," Strategy+Business, May 23, 2019. Accessed June 1, 2019, at https://www.strategy-business.com/article/Create-a-workplace-where-everyone-feels-comfortable-speaking-up?gko=7c8d3.

6. Elizabeth Kensinger, "New Study Suggests We Remember the Bad Times Better Than the Good," Association for Psychological Science, August 28, 2007. Accessed October 12, 2019, at https://www.psychologicalscience.org/news/releases/new-study-suggests-we-remember-the-bad-times-better-than-the-good.html.

7. Jake Herway, "How to Create a Culture of Psychological Safety," Gallup, December 7, 2017. Accessed October 28, 2019, at https://www.gallup.com/workplace/236198/create-culture-psychological-safety.aspx.

8. Peter Holland, Amanda Pyman, Brian Cooper, and Julian Teicher, "Employee Voice and Job Satisfaction in Australia: the Centrality of Voice," Wiley Online Library—HR Science Forum, January 26, 2011. Accessed October 11, 2019, at https://onlinelibrary.wiley.com/doi/abs/10.1002/hrm.20406.

9. Edmondson, *The Fearless Organization*, p. 8.

Chapter 4

1. Karin Hurt and David Dye, *Winning Well: A Manager's Guide to Getting Results without Losing Your Soul* (New York: AMACOM, 2016).

Chapter 5

1. Mark Nepo, *The Book of Awakening* (San Francisco: Red Wheel/Weiser, 2000), p. 217.

2. Smith, Weller, and Rock, "Create a Workplace Where Everyone Feels Comfortable Speaking Up."

Chapter 7

1. Alvin Toffler Quotes, BrainyQuote.com. Accessed January 6, 2020, at https://www.brainyquote.com/quotes/alvin_toffler_130763.

2. Henry King, "5 Ways that Standardization Can Lead to Innovation," Fast Company, August 3, 2011. Accessed October 10, 2019, at https://www.fastcompany.com/1664682/5-ways-that-standardization-can-lead-to-innovation.

Chapter 8

1. John Dore, "5 Keys to Unlock Innovation," London Business School, March 15, 2019. Accessed May 29, 2019, at https://www.london.edu/lbsr/5-keys-to-unlock-innovation.

Chapter 9

1. Adam Grant, "Why So Many Ideas Are Pitched as 'Uber for X,'" *Atlantic*, February 4, 2016. Accessed Jan 6, 2019, at https://www.theatlantic.com/business/archive/2016/02/adam-grant-originals-uber-for-x/459321/.

2. Mark Murphy, "Research Shows the Quickest Way to Build Trust with Employees," *Forbes*, June 17, 2018. Accessed October 9, 2019, at https://www.forbes.com/sites/markmurphy/2018/06/17/research-shows-the-quickest-way-to-build-trust-with-your-employees/#1d36cc816757.

Chapter 10

1. Amelia Earhart Quotes, BrainyQuote.com. Accessed January 6, 2020, at https://www.brainyquote.com/quotes/amelia_earhart_120932.

2. Eric Karlson, "Retailer Preference Index 2018: Grocery Edition," dunnhumby, January 15, 2018. Accessed October 15, 2019, at https://www.dunnhumby.com/resources/reports/retailer-preference-index-2018.

3. Stephen J. Dubner, "Should America Be Run by . . . Trader Joe's?" Freakonomics Radio, November 28, 2018. Accessed October 13, 2019, at http://freakonomics.com/podcast/trader-joes/.

4. "It's About the Values," Inside Trader Joe's Podcast, May 1, 2018. Accessed October 12, 2019, at https://www.traderjoes.com/TJ_CMS_Content/Images/Digin/pdfs/InsideTJs-Episode2-Transcript.pdf.

5. Deena Shanker and Lydia Mulvany, "The Curse of the Honeycrisp Apple," Bloomberg, November 8, 2018. Accessed October 12, 2019, at https://www.bloomberg.com/news/articles/2018-11-08/the-curse-of-the-honeycrisp-apple.

Chapter 11

1. J. R. R. Tolkien, *The Hobbit* (New York: Ballantine Books, 1965), p. 77.

2. Oxford Dictionaries, s.v. "galvanize." Accessed October 21, 2019, at https://www.lexico.com/en/definition/galvanize.

3. Brené Brown, *Rising Strong: How the Ability to Reset Transforms the Way We Live, Love, Parent, and Lead* (New York: Spiel-Grau, 2015), Kindle edition, p. 290.

Chapter 13

1. Fred Rogers, *A Beautiful Day in the Neighborhood* (New York: Penguin Books, 1994), p. 92.

2. Edmondson, *The Fearless Organization*, pp. 16–17.

3. Adam Grant, "Are You a Giver or a Taker?" TED, November 2016. Accessed October 17, 2019, at https://www.ted.com/talks/adam_grant_are_you_a_giver_or_a_taker/transcript?language=en.

4. Nicole Torres, "It's Better to Avoid a Toxic Employee Than to Hire a Superstar," *Harvard Business Review*, December 9, 2015. Accessed October 17, 2019, at https://hbr.org/2015/12/its-better-to-avoid-a-toxic-employee-than-hire-a-superstar.

5. Randall Beck and Jim Harter, "Managers Account for 70% of Variance in Employee Engagement," Gallup, April 21, 2015. Accessed August 2, 2019, at https://news.gallup.com/businessjournal/182792/managers-account-variance-employee-engagement.aspx.

6. "Ninety-Eight Percent of U.S. Managers Want Better Management Training," Cision, September 28, 2016. Accessed October 27, 2019, at http://www.prweb.com/releases/2016/09/prweb13719059.htm.

7. Ray Dalio, *Principles* (New York: Simon & Schuster, 2019), Kindle edition, p. 328.

8. Ray Dalio, "How to Build a Company Where the Best Ideas Win," TED, April 2017. Accessed October 20, 2019, at https://www.ted.com/talks/ray_dalio _how_to_build_a_company_where_the_best_ideas_win/transcript.

Chapter 14

1. Brene Brown, *The Gifts of Imperfection* (Center City, MN: Hazelden, 2010), p. 61.

Chapter 15

1. Linda Wagner-Martin, *Maya Angelou: Adventurous Spirit* (New York: Bloomsbury, 2016), p. 166.

Index

About the Authors

KARIN HURT is founder and CEO of Let's Grow Leaders, an international training company known for its innovative and practical approaches to leadership development. A former Verizon Wireless executive, she has more than two decades of experience in sales, customer service, and human resources. She was recently named to *Inc.'s* list of 100 Great Leadership Speakers.

DAVID DYE, president of Let's Grow Leaders, works with leaders to achieve transformational results without sacrificing their humanity. As a former executive and elected official, he inspires audiences with practical leadership inspiration you can use right away.

Their other books include: *Winning Well: A Manager's Guide to Getting Results—Without Losing Your Soul; Seven Things Your Team Needs to Hear You Say; Overcoming an Imperfect Boss,* and *Glowstone Peak.* Karin and David are dedicated to their philanthropic initiative, Winning Wells, which provides clean water wells to communities struggling with access to safe water throughout Southeast Asia.